T0021279

3RD EDITION

Birds *of* Michigan

Field Guide

Stan Tekiela

Adventure Publications
Cambridge, Minnesota

Dedication

To my wife, Katherine, and daughter, Abigail, with all my love.

Acknowledgments

Many thanks to the National Wildlife Refuge System along with state and local agencies, both public and private, for stewarding the lands that are critical to the many bird species we so love.

Edited by Sandy Livoti

Cover, book design and illustrations by Jonathan Norberg

Range maps produced by Anthony Hertzel

Cover photo: American Goldfinch by Stan Tekiela
All photos by Stan Tekiela except pg. 275 (juvenile) by **Rick and Nora Bowers**; pg. 192 (female) by **Kevin T. Karlson**; pp. 42 (female) and 295 by **Maslowski Wildlife Productions**; pg. 220 (displaying) by **Harmut Walter**; pp. 38 (juvenile), 141 (both juveniles), 230 (juvenile) and 232 (in-flight juvenile) by **Brian K. Wheeler**; and pp. 178 (female), 224 (main), 272 (in flight) and 288 (female) by **Jim Zipp**

To the best of the publisher's knowledge, all photos were of live birds. Some were photographed in a controlled condition.

15 14 13

Birds of Michigan Field Guide
First Edition 1999
Second Edition 2004
Third Edition 2019
Copyright © 1999, 2004 and 2019 by Stan Tekiela
Published by Adventure Publications
An imprint of AdventureKEEN
310 Garfield Street South
Cambridge, Minnesota 55008
(800) 678-7006
www.adventurepublications.net
All rights reserved
Printed in China
ISBN 978-1-59193-900-9 (pbk.); ISBN 978-1-59193-901-6 (ebook)

TABLE OF CONTENTS

WHAT'S NEW?

It is hard to believe that it's been over 20 years since the debut of Birds of Michigan Field Guide. This critically acclaimed guide has helped countless people identify and enjoy the birds that we love. Now, in this expanded third edition, *Birds of Michigan Field Guide* has many new and exciting changes and a fresh look, while retaining the same easy-to-use, familiar format.

To help you identify even more birds in Michigan, I have added six new species and am featuring 135 new color photographs. All of the range maps have been meticulously reviewed, and many updates have been made to reflect the ever-changing movements of the birds.

Everyone's favorite section, Stan's Notes, has been expanded to include even more natural history information. Compare sections have been updated to help ensure that you correctly identify your bird, and additional feeder information has been added to help with bird feeding. I hope you will enjoy this great new edition as you continue to learn about and appreciate our Michigan birds!

WHY WATCH BIRDS IN MICHIGAN?

Millions of people in Michigan have discovered bird feeding. Setting out feeders is a simple and enjoyable way to bring birds and their beauty closer to you. Watching birds at your feeders and listening to them often leads to a lifetime pursuit of bird identification. *Birds of Michigan Field Guide* is for those who want to identify the common birds of Michigan.

More than 1,100 species of birds are found in North America. In Michigan, upwards of 400 species of birds were documented throughout the years. These bird sightings were diligently recorded by hundreds of bird watchers and became part of the official state records. From these, I have chosen 118 of the most common birds of Michigan to include in this field guide.

Bird watching, also called birding, is one of the most popular activities in America. Its outstanding appeal in Michigan is due to unusually rich and abundant birdlife all around the state.

At more than 96,700 square miles (250,500 sq. km), Michigan is the eleventh-largest state in the country. Despite its large size, it has a population of only about 10 million. On average, that is only 174 people per square mile (67 per sq. km). Most are located in the southern portion of the Lower Peninsula.

Several distinct habitats in Michigan support different groups of birds. The state is roughly divided into two large peninsulas—a large Lower Peninsula (L.P.) and a smaller Upper Peninsula (U.P.). Over half of the land in Michigan is forested, especially in the U.P. Dotted in and among these vast tracts of forest are more than 6,000 lakes, each over 10 acres (4 ha) in size, as well as hundreds of miles of streams and rivers, and large tracts of high- and low-relief sand dunes.

Michigan's vegetation is highly varied and differs somewhat in the U.P. and L.P. The coniferous forests of the U.P. are mostly a mix of red and white pines. These evergreen woods are havens for birds such as Common Ravens, Evening Grosbeaks and Ruby-crowned Kinglets. Deciduous trees in the L.P. woods are a combination of oak, beech, ash and maple. Here you can find Gray Catbirds, House Wrens, Brown Thrashers and more.

Michigan is truly a Great Lakes state. It is bordered by four of the five Great Lakes and has more than 3,300 miles (5,300 km) of shoreline. Michigan has the second-longest shoreline in the United States—only Alaska has more coast! No point anywhere in Michigan is more than 85 miles (137 km) from one of the bordering Great Lakes.

Michigan has many major rivers, including the Kalamazoo, the Manistee, and the state's longest river, the Grand. Tall shade trees line the riverbanks and cool water flows through the river valleys, making them outstanding places to see birds. Here, Green Herons stalk the riverbanks in search of fish, aquatic insects and amphibians.

Complementing our wide-ranging seasonal weather, we have a wide range of birds to enjoy in each season. From the hawks migrating in the fall to the hummingbirds returning in spring, there is variety and excitement in birding at any time of year!

OBSERVATION STRATEGIES: TIPS TO IDENTIFY BIRDS

Identifying birds isn't as difficult as you might think. By simply following a few basic strategies, you can increase your chances of successfully identifying most birds that you see! One of the first and easiest things to do when you see a new bird is to note its color. This field guide is organized by color, so simply turn to the right color section to find it.

Next, note the size of the bird. A strategy to quickly estimate size is to compare different birds. Pick a small, a medium and a large bird. Select an American Robin as the medium bird. Measured from bill tip to tail tip, a robin is 10 inches (25 cm).

Now select two other birds, one smaller and one larger. Good choices are a House Sparrow, at about 6 inches (15 cm), and an American Crow, around 18 inches (45 cm). When you see a species you don't know, you can now quickly ask yourself, "Is it larger than a sparrow but smaller than a robin?" When you look in your field guide to identify your bird, you would check the species that are roughly 6–10 inches (15–25 cm). This will help to narrow your choices.

Next, note the size, shape and color of the bill. Is it long, short, thick, thin, pointed, blunt, curved or straight? Seed-eating birds, such as Northern Cardinals, have bills that are thick and strong enough to crack even the toughest seeds. Birds that sip nectar, such as Ruby-throated Hummingbirds, need long, thin bills to reach deep into flowers. Hawks and owls tear their prey with very sharp, curving bills. Sometimes, just noting the bill shape can help you decide whether the bird is a woodpecker, sparrow, grosbeak, blackbird or bird of prey.

Next, take a look around and note the habitat in which you see the bird. Is it wading in a marsh? Walking along a riverbank? Soaring in the sky? Is it perched high in the trees or hopping along the forest floor? Because of diet and habitat preferences, you'll often see robins hopping on the ground but not usually eating seeds at a feeder. Or you'll see a Blue Jay sitting on a tree branch but not climbing headfirst down a tree trunk, like a White-breasted Nuthatch.

Noticing what a bird is eating will give you another clue to help you identify the species. Feeding is a big part of any bird's life. Fully one-third of all bird activity revolves around searching for food, catching prey and eating.

While birds don't always follow all the rules of their diet, you can make some general assumptions. Northern Flickers, for instance, feed on ants and other insects, so you wouldn't expect to see them visiting a seed feeder. Other birds, such as Barn and Tree Swallows, eat flying insects and spend hours swooping and diving to catch a meal.

Sometimes you can identify a bird by the way it perches. Body posture can help you differentiate between an American Crow and a Red-tailed Hawk, for example. Crows lean forward over their feet on a branch, while hawks perch in a vertical position. Consider posture the next time you see an unidentified large bird in a tree.

Birds in flight are harder to identify, but noting the wing size and shape will help. Wing size is in direct proportion to body size, weight and type of flight. Wing shape determines if the bird flies fast and with precision, or slowly and less precisely. Barn Swallows, for instance, have short, pointed wings that slice through the air, propelling swift, accurate flight. Turkey Vultures have long, broad wings for soaring on warm updrafts of air. House Finches have short, rounded wings, helping them to flit through thick tangles of branches.

Some bird species have a unique pattern of flight that can help in identification. American Goldfinches, Pine Siskins and other finches fly in a distinctive undulating pattern that makes it look like they're riding a roller coaster.

While it's not easy to make all of these observations in the short time you often have to watch a "mystery" bird, practicing these identification methods will greatly expand your birding skills. To further improve your skills, seek the guidance of a more experienced birder who can answer your questions on the spot.

BIRD BASICS

It's easier to identify birds and communicate about them if you know the names of the different parts of a bird. For instance, it's more effective to use the word "crest" to indicate the set of extra-long feathers on top of a Northern Cardinal's head than to try to describe it.

The following illustration points out the basic parts of a bird. Because it is a composite of many birds, it shouldn't be confused with any actual bird.

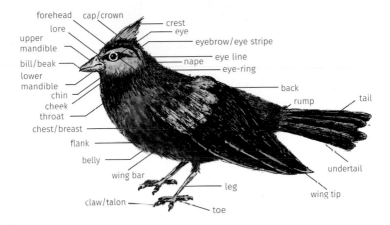

Bird Color Variables

No other animal has a color palette like a bird's. Brilliant blues, lemon-yellows, showy reds and iridescent greens are common in the bird world. In general, male birds are more colorful than their female counterparts. This helps males attract a mate, essentially saying, "Hey, look at me!" Color calls attention to a male's health as well. The better the condition of his feathers, the better his food source, territory and potential for mating.

Male and female birds that don't look like each other are called sexually dimorphic, meaning "two forms." Dimorphic females often have a nondescript dull color, as seen in Indigo Buntings. Muted tones help females hide during the weeks of motionless incubation and draw less attention to them when they're out feeding or taking a break from the rigors of raising the young.

The males of some species, such as the Downy Woodpecker, Blue Jay and Bald Eagle, look nearly identical to the females. In woodpeckers, the sexes are differentiated by only a red mark, or sometimes a yellow mark. Depending on the species, the mark may be on top of the head, on the face or nape of neck, or just behind the bill.

During the first year, juvenile birds often look like their mothers. Since brightly colored feathers are used mainly for attracting a mate, young non-breeding males don't have a need for colorful plumage. It's not until the first spring molt (or several years later, depending on the species) that young males obtain their breeding colors.

Both breeding and winter plumages are the result of molting. Molting is the process of dropping old, worn feathers and replacing them with new ones. All birds molt, typically twice a year, with the spring molt usually occurring in late winter. At this time, most birds produce their brighter breeding plumage, which lasts throughout the summer.

Winter plumage is the result of the late summer molt, which serves a couple of important functions. First, it adds feathers for warmth in the coming winter season. Second, in some species it produces feathers that tend to be drab in color, which helps to camouflage the birds and hide them from predators. The winter plumage of the male American Goldfinch, for example, is olive-brown, unlike its canary-yellow breeding color during summer. Luckily for us, some birds, such as the male Northern Cardinal, retain their bright summer colors all year long.

Bird Nests

Bird nests are a true feat of engineering. Imagine constructing a home that's strong enough to weather storms, large enough to hold your entire family, insulated enough to shelter them from cold and heat, and waterproof enough to keep out rain. Think about building it without blueprints or directions and using mainly your feet. Birds do this!

Before building, birds must select an appropriate site. In some species, such as the House Wren, the male picks out several potential sites and assembles small twigs in each. The "extra" nests, called dummy nests, discourage other birds from using any nearby cavities for their nests. The male takes the female around and shows her the choices. After choosing her favorite, she finishes the construction.

In other species, such as the Baltimore Oriole, the female selects the site and builds the nest, while the male offers an occasional suggestion. Each bird species has its own nest-building routine that is strictly followed.

As you can see in these illustrations, birds build a wide variety of nest types.

| ground
nest | platform
nest | cup
nest | pendulous
nest | cavity
nest |

Nesting material often consists of natural items found in the immediate area. Most nests consist of plant fibers (such as bark from grapevines), sticks, mud, dried grass, feathers, fur, or soft, fuzzy tufts from thistle. Some birds, including Ruby-throated Hummingbirds, use spiderwebs to glue nest materials together.

Transportation of nesting material is limited to the amount a bird can hold or carry. Birds must make many trips afield to gather enough material to complete a nest. Most nests take four days or more, and hundreds, if not thousands, of trips to build.

A **ground nest** can be a mound of vegetation on the ground or in the water. It can also be just a simple, shallow depression scraped in earth, stones or sand. Killdeer and Horned Larks scrape out ground nests without adding any nesting material.

The **platform nest** represents a much more complex type of construction. Typically built with twigs or sticks and branches, this nest forms a platform and has a depression in the center to nestle the eggs. Platform nests can be in trees, on cliffs, bridges, balconies, man-made platforms, and even in flower-pots. They often provide space for the adventurous young and function as a landing platform for the parents.

Mourning Doves and herons don't anchor their platform nests to trees, so these can tumble from branches during high winds and storms. Hawks, eagles, ospreys and other birds construct sturdier platform nests with their large sticks and branches.

Other platform nests are constructed on the ground with mud, grass and other vegetation from the area. Many waterfowl build platform nests on the ground near water or actually in the water. A **floating platform nest** moves with the water level, preventing the nest, eggs and birds from being flooded.

Three-quarters of all songbirds construct a **cup nest**, which is a modified platform nest. The supporting platform is built first and attached firmly to a tree, shrub, rock ledge or the ground.

Next, the sides are constructed with grass, small twigs, bark or leaves, which are woven together and often glued with mud for added strength. The inner cup can be lined with down feathers, animal fur or hair, or soft plant materials and is contoured last.

The **pendulous nest** is an unusual nest that looks like a sock hanging from a branch. Attached to the end of small branches of trees, this unique nest is inaccessible to most predators and often waves wildly in a breeze.

Woven tightly with plant fibers, the pendulous nest is strong, watertight and takes up to a week to build. A small opening at the top or on the side allows parents access to the grass-lined interior. More commonly used by tropical birds, this complex nest has also been mastered by orioles and kinglets. It must be one heck of a ride to be inside one of these nests during a windy spring thunderstorm!

The **cavity nest** is used by many species of birds, most notably woodpeckers and owls. A cavity nest is often excavated in a branch or tree trunk and offers shelter from storms, sun, cold and predators. A small entrance hole in a tree can lead to a nest chamber, for example, up to a safe 10 inches (25 cm) deep.

Typically made by woodpeckers, cavity nests are usually used only once by the builder. Nest cavities can be used for many subsequent years by such species as mergansers or blue-birds. Kingfishers, on the other hand, can dig a tunnel up to 4 feet (1 m) long in a riverbank. The nest chamber at the end of the tunnel is already well insulated, so it's usually only sparsely lined.

One of the most clever of all nests is the **no nest**, or daycare nest. Parasitic birds, such as Brown-headed Cowbirds, don't build their own nests. Instead, the egg-laden female searches out the nest of another bird and sneaks in to lay an egg while the host mother isn't looking.

A mother cowbird wastes no energy building a nest only to have it raided by a predator. Laying her eggs in the nests of other birds transfers the responsibility of raising her young to the host. When she lays her eggs in several nests, the chances increase that at least one of her babies will live to maturity.

Who Builds the Nest?

Generally, the female bird constructs the nest. She gathers the materials and does the building, with an occasional visit from her mate to check on progress. In some species, both parents contribute equally to nest building. The male bird may forage for sticks, grass or mud, but it is the female that often fashions the nest. Only rarely does a male build a nest by himself.

Fledging

Fledging is the interval between hatching and flight, or leaving the nest. Some species of birds leave the nest within hours of hatching (precocial), but it may be weeks before they are able to fly. This is common in waterfowl and shorebirds.

Baby birds that hatch naked and blind need to stay in the nest for a few weeks (altricial). Baby birds that are still in the nest are nestlings. Until birds start to fly, they are called fledglings.

Why Birds Migrate

Why do so many species of birds migrate? The short answer is simple—food. Birds migrate to locations with abundant food, as it is easier to breed where there is food than where it is not. Purple Martins, for instance, are **complete migrators** that fly from the tropics of South America to nest in the forests of North America, where billions of newly hatched insects are available to feed to their young.

Other migrators, such as some birds of prey, migrate back to northern regions in spring. In these locations, they hunt mice, voles and other small rodents, which are beginning to breed.

Complete migrators have a set time and pattern of migration. Every year at nearly the same time, they head to a specific wintering ground. Complete migrators may travel great distances, sometimes 15,000 miles (24,100 km) or more in one year.

Complete migration doesn't necessarily mean flying from the frozen northland to a tropical destination. Dark-eyed Juncos, for example, are complete migrators that move from the far reaches of Canada to spend the winter here in cold and snowy Michigan. This trip is still considered complete migration.

Complete migrators have many interesting aspects. In spring, males often leave a few weeks before the females, arriving early to scope out possibilities for nesting sites and food sources, and to begin to defend territories. The females arrive several weeks later. In many species, the females and their young leave earlier in the fall, often up to four weeks before the adult males.

Other species, such as the American Goldfinch, are **partial migrators**. These birds usually wait until their food supplies dwindle before flying south. Unlike complete migrators, partial migrators move only far enough south, or sometimes east and west, to find abundant food. In some years it might be only a few hundred miles, while in other years it can be as much as a thousand. This kind of migration, dependent on weather and the availability of food, is sometimes called seasonal movement.

Unlike the predictable complete migrators or partial migrators, **irruptive migrators** can move every third to fifth year or, in some cases, in consecutive years. These migrations are triggered when times are really tough and food is scarce. Pine Grosbeaks are irruptive migrators. They leave their normal northern range in search of more food or in response to overpopulation.

Many other birds don't migrate at all. Black-capped Chickadees, for example, are **non-migrators** that remain in their habitat all year long and just move around as necessary to find food.

How Do Birds Migrate?

One of the many secrets of migration is fat. While most people are fighting the ongoing battle of the bulge, birds intentionally gorge themselves to gain as much fat as possible without losing the ability to fly. Fat provides the greatest amount of energy per unit of weight. In the same way that your car needs gas, birds are propelled by fat and stalled without it.

During long migratory flights, fat deposits are used up quickly, and birds need to stop to "refuel." This is when backyard bird feeding stations and undeveloped, natural spaces around our towns and cities are especially important. Some birds require up to 2–3 days of constant feeding to build their fat reserves before continuing their seasonal trip.

Many birds, such as most eagles, hawks, ospreys, falcons and vultures, migrate during the day. Larger birds can hold more body fat, go longer without eating and take longer to migrate. These birds glide along on rising columns of warm air, called thermals, which hold them aloft while they slowly make their way north or south. They generally rest at night and hunt early in the morning before the sun has a chance to warm the land and create good soaring conditions. Daytime migrators use a combination of landforms, rivers, and the rising and setting sun to guide them in the right direction.

The majority of small birds, called passerines, migrate at night. Studies show that some use the stars to navigate. Others use the setting sun, and still others, such as pigeons, use Earth's magnetic field to guide them north or south.

While flying at night may not seem like a good idea, it's actually safer. First, there are fewer avian predators hunting for birds at night. Second, night travel allows time during the day to find food in unfamiliar surroundings. Third, wind patterns at night tend to be flat, or laminar. Flat winds don't have the turbulence of daytime winds and can help push the smaller birds along.

HOW TO USE THIS GUIDE

To help you quickly and easily identify birds, this field guide is organized by color. Refer to the color key on the first page, simply note the color of the bird and turn to that section. For example, the male Rose-breasted Grosbeak is black-and-white with a red patch on his chest. Because the bird is mostly black-and-white, it will be found in the black-and-white section.

Each color section is also arranged by size, generally with the smaller birds first. Sections may also incorporate the average size in a range, which, in some cases, reflects size differences between male and female birds. Flip through the pages in the color section to find the bird. If you already know the name of the bird, check the index for the page number.

In some species, the male and female are very different in color. In others, the breeding and winter plumage colors differ. These species will have an inset photograph with a page reference and will be found in two color sections.

You will find a variety of information in the bird description sections. To learn more, turn to the sample on pp. 20–21.

Range Maps

Range maps are included for each bird. Colored areas indicate where the bird is frequently found. The colors represent the presence of a species during a specific season, not the density, or amount, of birds in the area. Green is used for summer, blue for winter, red for year-round and yellow for migration.

While every effort has been made to depict accurate ranges, these actually change on an ongoing basis due to a variety of factors. Changing weather, habitat, species abundance and vital resources, such as the availability of food and water, can affect local populations, migration and movements, causing birds to be found in areas that are atypical for the species. So please use the maps as intended, as general guides only.

female
pg. 105

male

Common Name

Range Map *Scientific name* **Color Indicator**

YEAR-ROUND
SUMMER
MIGRATION
WINTER

Size: measurement is from head to tip of tail; may include the wingspan

Male: brief description of the male bird; may include breeding, winter or other plumages

Female: brief description of the female bird, which is sometimes different from the male

Juvenile: brief description of the juvenile bird, which often looks like the adult female

Nest: kind of nest the bird builds to raise its young; who builds it; number of broods per year

Eggs: number of eggs you might expect to see in a nest; color and marking

Incubation: average days the parents spend incubating the eggs; who does the incubation

Fledging: average days the young spend in the nest after hatching but before they leave the nest; who does the most "childcare" and feeding

Migration: complete (consistent, seasonal), non-migrator, partial (seasonal, destination varies), irruptive (unpredictable, depends on the food supply); additional comments

Food: what the bird eats most of the time (e.g., seeds, insects, fruit, nectar, small mammals, fish); if it typically comes to a bird feeding station

Compare: notes about other birds that look similar and the pages on which they can be found; may include extra information to aid identification

Stan's Notes: Interesting gee-whiz natural history information. This could be something to look or listen for, or something to help positively identify the bird. Also includes remarkable features.

female
pg. 127

male

Eastern Towhee
Pipilo erythrophthalmus

SUMMER

Size: 7–8" (18–20 cm)

Male: Mostly black with dirty red-brown sides and a white belly. Long black tail with a white tip. Short, stout, pointed bill and rich red eyes. White wing patches flash in flight.

Female: similar to male, but brown instead of black

Juvenile: light brown with heavily streaked head, chest and belly, a long dark tail with a white tip

Nest: cup; female builds; 2 broods per year

Eggs: 3–4; cream-white with brown markings

Incubation: 12–13 days; female incubates

Fledging: 10–12 days; male and female feed young

Migration: complete, to southern states, Mexico, Central and South America

Food: insects, seeds, fruit; visits ground feeders

Compare: American Robin (pg. 219) lacks the white belly. Gray Catbird (pg. 217) lacks the black head and rusty sides. The Common Grackle (pg. 31) lacks a white belly and has a long, thin bill. The male Rose-breasted Grosbeak (pg. 47) has a rosy patch on its chest.

Stan's Notes: Named for its distinctive "tow-hee" call, given by both sexes. Known mostly for its other characteristic call, which sounds like "drink-your-tea!" Will hop backward with both feet (bilateral scratching), raking up leaf litter to locate insects and seeds. The female does the brooding. Male feeds the young most of the time. In southern coastal states, some individuals have red eyes; others have white eyes. Only the red-eyed variety is seen in Michigan.

female
pg. 129

male

SUMMER

Brown-headed Cowbird
Molothrus ater

Size: 7½" (19 cm)

Male: A glossy black bird with a chocolate-brown head and pointed, sharp gray bill. Dark eyes.

Female: dull brown with a pointed gray bill

Juvenile: similar to female, but dull gray plumage with a streaked chest

Nest: no nest; lays eggs in the nests of other birds

Eggs: 5–7; white with brown markings

Incubation: 10–13 days; host birds incubate the eggs

Fledging: 10–11 days; host birds feed the young

Migration: complete, to southern states

Food: insects, seeds; will come to seed feeders

Compare: Male Red-winged Blackbird (pg. 29) is slightly larger and has red-and-yellow patches on its upper wings. The Common Grackle (pg. 31) has a long tail and lacks the brown head. European Starling (pg. 27) has a shorter tail.

Stan's Notes: Cowbirds are members of the blackbird family. Known as brood parasites, Brown-headed Cowbirds are the only parasitic birds in Michigan. Brood parasites lay their eggs in the nests of other birds, leaving the host birds to raise their young. Cowbirds are known to have laid their eggs in the nests of over 200 species of birds. While some birds reject cowbird eggs, most incubate them and raise the young, even to the exclusion of their own. Look for warblers and other birds feeding young birds twice their own size. Named "Cowbird" for its habit of following bison and cattle herds to feed on insects flushed up by the animals.

25

winter

breeding

European Starling
Sturnus vulgaris

YEAR-ROUND

Size: 7½" (19 cm)

Male: Glittering, iridescent purplish-black in spring and summer, duller and speckled with white in fall and winter. Long, pointed yellow bill in spring, gray in fall. Pointed wings. Short tail.

Female: same as male

Juvenile: similar to adult, with grayish-brown plumage and a streaked chest

Nest: cavity; male and female line cavity; 2 broods per year

Eggs: 4–6; bluish with brown markings

Incubation: 12–14 days; female and male incubate

Fledging: 18–20 days; female and male feed the young

Migration: non-migrator to partial; some will move to southern states

Food: insects, seeds, fruit; visits seed or suet feeders

Compare: The Common Grackle (pg. 31) has a long tail. Male Brown-headed Cowbird (pg. 25) has a brown head. Look for the shiny dark feathers to help identify the European Starling.

Stan's Notes: One of our most numerous songbirds. Mimics the songs of up to 20 bird species and imitates sounds, including the human voice. Jaws are more powerful when opening rather than closing, enabling the bird to pry open crevices to find insects. Often displaces woodpeckers, chickadees and other cavity-nesting birds. Large families gather with blackbirds in the fall. Not a native bird; 100 starlings were introduced to New York City in 1890–91 from Europe. Bill changes color with the seasons in spring and fall.

female
pg. 137

male

SUMMER

Red-winged Blackbird
Agelaius phoeniceus

Size:	8½" (21.5 cm)
Male:	Jet-black with red-and-yellow patches on the upper wings (epaulets). Pointed black bill.
Female:	heavily streaked brown bird with a pointed brown bill and white eyebrows
Juvenile:	same as female
Nest:	cup; female builds; 2–3 broods per year
Eggs:	3–4; bluish-green with brown markings
Incubation:	10–12 days; female incubates
Fledging:	11–14 days; female and male feed the young
Migration:	complete, to southern states, Mexico and Central America
Food:	seeds, insects; visits seed and suet feeders
Compare:	The male Brown-headed Cowbird (pg. 25) is smaller, glossier and has a brown head. The bold red-and-yellow epaulets distinguish the male Red-winged from all other blackbirds.

Stan's Notes: One of the most widespread and numerous birds in Michigan. Found around marshes, wetlands, lakes and rivers. It is a sure sign of spring when these birds return home. Flocks with as many as 10,000 birds have been reported. Males arrive before the females and sing to defend their territory. The male repeats his call from the top of a cattail while showing off his red-and-yellow shoulder patches. The female chooses a mate and often builds her nest over shallow water in a thick stand of cattails. The male can be aggressive when defending the nest. Feeds mostly on seeds in spring and fall, and insects throughout the summer.

Common Grackle
Quiscalus quiscula

SUMMER

Size: 11–13" (28–33 cm)

Male: Large iridescent blackbird with a bluish-black head, purplish-brown body, long black tail, a long, thin bill and bright golden eyes.

Female: similar to male, only smaller and duller

Juvenile: similar to female

Nest: cup; female builds; 2 broods per year

Eggs: 4–5; greenish-white with brown markings

Incubation: 13–14 days; female incubates

Fledging: 16–20 days; female and male feed the young

Migration: complete, to southern states

Food: fruit, seeds, insects; will come to seed and suet feeders

Compare: European Starling (pg. 27) is much smaller with a shorter tail, and it has a yellow bill during the breeding season. The male Red-winged Blackbird (pg. 29) has bright red-and-yellow shoulder patches.

Stan's Notes: Usually nests in small colonies of up to 75 pairs but travels with other blackbird species in large flocks. Known to feed in farm fields. The common name is derived from the Latin word *gracula*, meaning "to croak," for its loud, raspy call. The male holds his tail in a deep V shape during flight. The flight pattern is usually level, as opposed to an undulating movement. Unlike most birds, it has larger muscles for opening its mouth (rather than for closing it), enabling it to pry crevices apart to find hidden insects.

in flight

American Crow
Corvus brachyrhynchos

YEAR-ROUND

Size: 18" (45 cm)

Male: All-black bird with a black bill, legs and feet. Can have a purple sheen in direct sunlight.

Female: same as male

Juvenile: same as adult

Nest: platform; female builds; 1 brood per year

Eggs: 4–6; bluish-to-olive with brown markings

Incubation: 18 days; female incubates

Fledging: 28–35 days; female and male feed the young

Migration: non-migrator to partial; some will move into cities during winter

Food: fruit, insects, mammals, fish, carrion; comes to seed and suet feeders

Compare: The Common Raven (pg. 37) has a larger bill, shaggy throat feathers, a deep, raspy call, and a wedged tail, as seen in flight. Look for the glossy black plumage and squared tail to help identify the American Crow.

Stan's Notes: A familiar bird, found in all habitats. Imitates other birds and human voices. One of the smartest of all birds and very social, often entertaining itself by provoking chases with other birds. Eats roadkill but rarely hit by vehicles. Can live up to 20 years. Often reuses its nest every year if not taken over by a Great Horned Owl. Unmated birds, known as helpers, help to raise the young. Extended families roost together at night, dispersing daily to hunt. Cannot soar on thermals. Flaps constantly and glides downward. Gathers in huge communal flocks of up to 10,000 birds in winter.

in flight

Common Raven
Corvus corax

Size: 22–27" (56–69 cm)

Male: Large all-black bird with a shaggy beard of feathers on throat and chin. Large black bill. Large wedge-shaped tail, best seen in flight.

Female: same as male

Juvenile: same as adult

Nest: platform; female and male build; 1 brood per year

Eggs: 4–6; pale green with brown markings

Incubation: 18–21 days; female incubates

Fledging: 38–44 days; female and male feed the young

Migration: non-migrator to partial; will move around in search of food

Food: insects, fruit, small animals, carrion

Compare: The American Crow (pg. 35), is smaller and lacks shaggy throat feathers. The Raven glides on flat, outstretched wings, unlike the slight V-shaped wing pattern of the Crow. Listen for the Raven's deep, raspy call to distinguish it from the higher-pitched call of the Crow.

Stan's Notes: Considered by some people to be the smartest of all birds. Known for its aerial acrobatics and long swooping dives. Sometimes scavenges with crows and gulls. A cooperative hunter that often communicates the location of a good source of food to other ravens. Known to follow wolf packs around to feed on their kills. Most start to breed at 3–4 years. Complex courtship includes grabbing bills, preening each other and cooing. Long-term pair bond. Uses the same nest site for many years.

soaring

juvenile

SUMMER

Turkey Vulture
Cathartes aura

Size: 26–32" (66–81 cm); up to 6-ft. wingspan

Male: Large black bird with a naked red head and legs. In flight, wings are two-toned with a black leading edge and a gray trailing edge. Wing tips end in finger-like projections. Tail is long and squared. Ivory bill.

Female: same as male, only slightly smaller

Juvenile: similar to adults, with a gray-to-blackish head and bill

Nest: no nest, or minimal nest on a cliff or in a cave, sometimes in a hollow tree; 1 brood per year

Eggs: 1–3; white with brown markings

Incubation: 38–41 days; female and male incubate

Fledging: 66–88 days; female and male feed the young

Migration: complete, to southern states, Mexico, Central and South America

Food: carrion; parents regurgitate to feed the young

Compare: Bald Eagle (pg. 71) is much larger and lacks two-toned wings. Look for the obvious naked red head to identify the Turkey Vulture.

Stan's Notes: The naked head reduces the risk of feather fouling (picking up diseases) from contact with carcasses. It has a strong bill for tearing apart flesh. Unlike hawks and eagles, it has weak feet more suited for walking than grasping. One of the few birds with a developed sense of smell. Mostly mute, making only grunts and groans. Holds its wings in an upright V shape in flight. Teeters from wing tip to wing tip as it soars and hovers. Seen in trees with wings outstretched, sunning itself and drying after a rain.

in flight

juvenile

crests

drying

Double-crested Cormorant
Phalacrocorax auritus

SUMMER MIGRATION

Size: 31–35" (79–89 cm); up to 4⅓-ft. wingspan

Male: Large black waterbird with unusual blue eyes and a long, snake-like neck. Large gray bill with yellow at the base and a hooked tip.

Female: same as male

Juvenile: lighter brown with a grayish chest and neck

Nest: platform; male and female build; 1 brood per year

Eggs: 3–4; bluish-white without markings

Incubation: 25–29 days; female and male incubate

Fledging: 37–42 days; male and female feed the young

Migration: complete, to southern states, Mexico and Central America

Food: small fish, aquatic insects

Compare: The Turkey Vulture (pg. 39) also spreads out its wings to dry in the sun, but it has a naked red head. The American Coot (pg. 33) has a duck-like white bill. Look for the long, snake-like neck and large, hooked bill to help identify the Cormorant.

Stan's Notes: Flies in a large V formation or a straight line. Usually roosts in large colonies in trees near water. Swims underwater to catch fish, holding its wings at its sides. Lacks the oil gland that keeps feathers from becoming waterlogged. To dry off, it strikes an upright pose with wings outstretched, facing the sun. Gives grunts, pops and groans. Named "Double-crested" for the two crests on its head, which are not often seen. "Cormorant" is a contraction from *corvus marinus*, meaning "crow" or "raven," and "of the sea."

41

male

female

Black-and-white Warbler

Mniotilta varia

SUMMER
MIGRATION

Size: 5" (13 cm)

Male: Small bird with zebra-like striping and a black-and-white striped crown. Black cheek patch and chin. White belly.

Female: duller than the male and lacks a black cheek patch and chin

Juvenile: similar to female

Nest: cup; female builds; 1 brood per year

Eggs: 4–5; white with brown markings

Incubation: 10–11 days; female incubates

Fledging: 9–12 days; female and male feed the young

Migration: complete, to Florida, Mexico, Central and South America

Food: insects

Compare: Climbs down tree trunks headfirst, like the White-breasted Nuthatch (pg. 199) and Red-breasted Nuthatch (pg. 195). Look for a small black-and-white bird climbing down trees to identify the Black-and-white Warbler.

Stan's Notes: This is the only warbler species that moves down tree trunks headfirst. Look for it searching for insect eggs in the bark of large trees. Its song sounds like a slowly turning, squeaky wheel going around and around. Female performs a distraction dance to draw predators away from the nest. Constructs its nest on the ground, concealing it under dead leaves or at the base of a tree. Found in a variety of habitats. Can be one of the more common warbler species during migration in both spring and fall.

male

female

YEAR-ROUND

Downy Woodpecker
Dryobates pubescens

Size: 6" (15 cm)

Male: A small woodpecker with a white belly and black-and-white spotted wings. Red mark on the back of head and a white stripe down the back. Short black bill.

Female: same as male, but lacks a red mark on head

Juvenile: same as female, some have a red mark near the forehead

Nest: cavity with a round entrance hole; male and female excavate; 1 brood per year

Eggs: 3–5; white without markings

Incubation: 11–12 days; female incubates during the day, male incubates at night

Fledging: 20–25 days; male and female feed the young

Migration: non-migrator

Food: insects, seeds; visits suet and seed feeders

Compare: Hairy Woodpecker (pg. 51) is larger. Look for the shorter, thinner bill to identify the Downy.

Stan's Notes: Abundant and widespread where trees are present. This is perhaps the most common woodpecker in the U.S. Stiff tail feathers help to brace it like a tripod as it clings to a tree. Like other woodpeckers, it has a long, barbed tongue to pull insects from tiny places. Mates drum on branches or hollow logs to announce territory, which is rarely larger than 5 acres (2 ha). Repeats a high-pitched "peek-peek" call. Nest cavity is wider at the bottom than at the top and is lined with fallen woodchips. Male performs most of the brooding. During winter, it will roost in a cavity. Undulates in flight.

female
pg. 125

male

Rose-breasted Grosbeak
Pheucticus ludovicianus

SUMMER

Size: 7–8" (18–20 cm)

Male: A plump black-and-white bird with a large, triangular rose patch in the center of breast. Wing linings are rose-red. Large ivory bill.

Female: heavily streaked bird with obvious white eyebrows and orange-to-yellow wing linings

Juvenile: similar to female

Nest: cup; female and male construct; 1–2 broods per year

Eggs: 3–5; blue-green with brown markings

Incubation: 13–14 days; female and male incubate

Fledging: 9–12 days; female and male feed the young

Migration: complete, to Mexico, Central America and South America

Food: insects, seeds, fruit; comes to seed feeders

Compare: Male is very distinctive with no look-alikes. Look for the rose breast patch to identify.

Stan's Notes: Seen in small groups. Prefers a mature deciduous forest for nesting. Both sexes sing, but the male sings much louder and clearer. Sings a rich, robin-like song with a chip note in the tune. "Grosbeak" refers to the thick, strong bill, which is used to crush seeds. The rose patch varies in size and shape in each male. Males have white wing patches that flash during flight. Males arrive at the breeding grounds a few days before the females. Several males will come to seed feeders together in spring. When the females arrive, males become territorial and reduce their feeder visits. After fledging, young grosbeaks visit feeders with the adults. Makes short flights from tree to tree with rapid wingbeats.

male

female

Yellow-bellied Sapsucker
Sphyrapicus varius

SUMMER
MIGRATION

Size: 8–9" (20–23 cm)

Male: Checkered back with a red forehead, crown and chin. Yellow-to-tan on chest and belly. White wing patches, seen flashing in flight.

Female: similar to male, but has a white chin

Juvenile: similar to female, but dull brown and lacks any red markings

Nest: cavity; female and male excavate, often in a live tree; 1 brood per year

Eggs: 5–6; white without markings

Incubation: 12–13 days; female incubates during the day, male incubates at night

Fledging: 25–29 days; female and male feed the young

Migration: complete, to southern states, Mexico and Central America

Food: insects, tree sap; comes to suet feeders

Compare: The Red-headed Woodpecker (pg. 53) has an all-red head. Look for the red chin and crown to identify the male Sapsucker, and the white chin and red crown to identify the female.

Stan's Notes: Found in small woods, forests, and suburban and rural areas. Drills holes in horizontal rows in trees to bleed the sap. Oozing sap attracts bugs, which it also eats. Defends its sapping sites from other birds that try to drink from the taps. Does not suck sap; rather, it laps the sticky liquid with its long, bristly tongue. A quiet bird with few vocalizations but will meow like a cat. Drums on hollow tree branches, but unlike other woodpeckers, its rhythm is irregular. Makes short undulating flights with rapid wingbeats.

male

female

YEAR-ROUND

Hairy Woodpecker
Dryobates villosus

Size:	9" (23 cm)
Male:	A black-and-white woodpecker with a white belly. Black wings with rows of white spots. White stripe down the back. Long black bill. Red mark on the back of head.
Female:	same as male, but lacks a red mark on head
Juvenile:	grayer version of the female
Nest:	cavity with an oval entrance hole; female and male excavate; 1 brood per year
Eggs:	3–6; white without markings
Incubation:	11–15 days; female incubates during the day, male incubates at night
Fledging:	28–30 days; male and female feed the young
Migration:	non-migrator
Food:	insects, nuts and seeds; will come to suet and seed feeders
Compare:	Much larger than the Downy Woodpecker (pg. 45) and has a much longer bill, nearly equal to the width of its head.

Stan's Notes: A common bird in wooded backyards. Announces its arrival with a sharp chirp before landing on feeders. Responsible for eating many destructive forest insects. Uses its barbed tongue to extract insects from trees. Tiny bristle-like feathers at the base of the bill protect the nostrils from wood dust. Drums on hollow logs, branches or stovepipes in spring to announce territory. Often prefers to excavate nest cavities in live aspen trees. Excavates a larger, more oval-shaped entrance than the round entrance hole of the Downy Woodpecker. Makes short flights from tree to tree.

juvenile

YEAR-ROUND
SUMMER

Red-headed Woodpecker

Melanerpes erythrocephalus

Size: 9" (23 cm)

Male: All-red head with a solid black back. Black wings with large white wing patches, seen flashing in flight. Black tail. White chest, belly and rump. Gray legs and bill.

Female: same as male

Juvenile: grayish-brown head and white chest

Nest: cavity; male excavates with some help from the female; 1 brood per year

Eggs: 4–5; white without markings

Incubation: 12–13 days; female and male incubate

Fledging: 27–30 days; female and male feed the young

Migration: partial migrator to complete; will move to areas with an abundant supply of nuts

Food: insects, nuts, fruit; visits suet and seed feeders

Compare: No other woodpecker in Michigan has an all-red head. Pileated Woodpecker (pg. 65) is the only other woodpecker with a solid black back, but it has a partial red head.

Stan's Notes: This is one of the few non-dimorphic woodpeckers, with males and females that look alike. Bill is strong enough to excavate a nest cavity only in soft, dead trees. Prefers open woodlands or woodland edges with many dead or rotting branches. Nests later than its close relative, the Red-bellied Woodpecker, and will often take its cavity, if vacant. Unlike other woodpeckers, which use nest cavities just once briefly, may use the same cavity for several years in a row. Often perches on top of dead snags. Stores acorns and other nuts. Gives a shrill, hoarse "churr" call.

male

female

YEAR-ROUND

Red-bellied Woodpecker
Melanerpes carolinus

Size: 9–9½" (23–24 cm)

Male: Black-and-white "zebra-backed" woodpecker with a white rump. Red crown extends down the nape of neck. Tan chest. Pale red tinge on the belly, often hard to see.

Female: same as male, but has a light gray crown and a red nape

Juvenile: gray version of adults; lacks a red crown and red nape

Nest: cavity; female and male excavate; 1 brood per year

Eggs: 4–5; white without markings

Incubation: 12–14 days; female incubates during the day, male incubates at night

Fledging: 24–27 days; female and male feed the young

Migration: non-migrator; moves around to find food

Food: insects, nuts, fruit; visits suet and seed feeders

Compare: Similar to the Northern Flicker (pg. 149) and Yellow-bellied Sapsucker (pg. 49). Look for the zebra-striped back to help identify the Red-bellied Woodpecker.

Stan's Notes: Likes shady woodlands, forest edges and backyards. Digs holes in rotten wood to find spiders, centipedes, beetles and more. Hammers acorns and berries into crevices of trees for winter food. Returns to the same tree to excavate a new nest below that of the previous year. Undulating flight with rapid wingbeats. Gives a loud "querrr" call and a low "chug-chug-chug." Named for the pale red tinge on its belly. Expanding its range all over the country.

female
pg. 155

male

Bufflehead
Bucephala albeola

MIGRATION

Size: 13–15" (33–38 cm)

Male: A small, striking duck with white sides and a black back. Greenish-purple head, iridescent in bright sun, with a large white head patch.

Female: brownish-gray with a dark brown head and white cheek patch behind the eyes

Juvenile: similar to female

Nest: cavity; female lines an old woodpecker hole; 1 brood per year

Eggs: 8–10; ivory-to-olive without markings

Incubation: 29–31 days; female incubates

Fledging: 50–55 days; female leads the young to food

Migration: complete, to southern states, Mexico and Central America

Food: aquatic insects, crustaceans, mollusks

Compare: Male Hooded Merganser (pg. 61) is larger and has rust-brown sides. Look for the large white bonnet-like patch on a greenish-purple head to help identify the male Bufflehead.

Stan's Notes: A small, common diving duck, almost always seen in small groups or with other duck species on rivers, ponds and lakes. Nests in vacant woodpecker holes. When cavities in trees are scarce, known to use a burrow in an earthen bank or will use a nest box. Lines the cavity with fluffy down feathers. Unlike other ducks, the young stay in the nest for up to two days before they venture out with their mothers. The female is very territorial and remains with the same mate for many years.

female
pg. 167

male

SUMMER
MIGRATION

Ring-necked Duck
Aythya collaris

Size: 16–19" (41–48 cm)

Male: A striking duck with a black head, chest and back and light gray-to-white sides. Blue bill with a bold white ring and thinner ring at the base. Peaked head with a sloped forehead.

Female: brown with a darker brown back and crown, light brown sides, gray face, white eye-ring, white ring around the bill, peaked head

Juvenile: similar to female

Nest: ground; female builds; 1 brood per year

Eggs: 8–10; olive-to-brown without markings

Incubation: 26–27 days; female incubates

Fledging: 49–56 days; female teaches the young to feed

Migration: complete, to southern states

Food: aquatic plants and insects

Compare: Male Bufflehead (pg. 57) is smaller and has a large white head patch. Look for the blue bill with an obvious white ring to identify the male Ring-necked Duck.

Stan's Notes: Often seen in pairs in larger freshwater lakes. Usually in small flocks. A diving duck, watch for it to dive underwater to forage for food. Springs up off the water to take flight. It has a distinctive tall, peaked head with a sloped forehead. Flattens its crown when diving. Male gives a quick series of grating barks and grunts. Female gives high-pitched peeps. Named "Ring-necked" for its cinnamon collar, which is nearly impossible to see in the field. Also called Ring-billed Duck due to the white ring on its bill.

female
pg. 169

male

SUMMER

Hooded Merganser
Lophodytes cucullatus

Size: 16–19" (41–48 cm)

Male: Black-and-white with rust-brown sides. Crest "hood" raises to show a large white patch on each side of the head. Long, thin black bill.

Female: brown-and-rust with ragged rust-red hair and a long, thin brown bill

Juvenile: similar to female

Nest: cavity; female lines an old woodpecker cavity or a nest box near water; 1 brood per year

Eggs: 10–12; white without markings

Incubation: 32–33 days; female incubates

Fledging: 71 days; female feeds the young

Migration: complete, to southern states

Food: small fish, aquatic insects and crustaceans (especially crayfish)

Compare: Male Bufflehead (pg. 57) is smaller and has white sides. Male Wood Duck (pg. 245) has a green head. The male Common Merganser (pg. 253) is much larger. Look for the large white patch on the sides of the head and rust-brown sides to identify the male Hoodie.

Stan's Notes: A small diving duck, found in shallow ponds, sloughs, lakes and rivers. Usually in small groups. Quick, low flight across the water, with fast wingbeats. Male has a deep, rolling call. Female gives a hoarse quack. Nests in wooded areas. Female will lay some eggs in the nests of other mergansers, goldeneyes or Wood Ducks (egg dumping), resulting in 20–25 eggs in some nests. Rarely, she shares a nest, sitting with a Wood Duck.

female
pg. 173

male

Common Goldeneye
Bucephala clangula

SUMMER
MIGRATION
WINTER

Size: 18–20" (45–51 cm)

Male: A mostly white duck with a black back and a large, puffy green head. Large white spot on the face. Bright golden eyes. Dark bill.

Female: large dark brown head, gray body, white collar, bright golden eyes and yellow-tipped dark bill

Juvenile: same as female, but has a dark bill

Nest: cavity; female lines an old woodpecker hole; 1 brood per year

Eggs: 8–10; light green without markings

Incubation: 28–32 days; female incubates

Fledging: 56–59 days; female leads the young to food

Migration: complete, to southern states and Mexico

Food: aquatic plants, insects, fish, mollusks

Compare: Male Bufflehead (pg. 57) is smaller and has a large white patch on the back of its head. Look for the distinctive white spot on the sides of the face and golden eyes to identify the male Common Goldeneye.

Stan's Notes: Known for the loud whistling sound produced by its wings during flight. During late winter and early spring, the male performs elaborate mating displays that include throwing his head back and calling a raspy note. Female will lay some of her eggs in other goldeneye nests or in the nests of other species (egg dumping), causing some mothers to incubate as many as 30 eggs in a brood. Named for its obvious bright golden eyes.

63

male

female

Pileated Woodpecker
Dryocopus pileatus

YEAR-ROUND

Size: 19" (48 cm)

Male: A crow-sized woodpecker with a black back and bold red forehead, crest and mustache. Long gray bill. White leading edge of wings flash brightly during flight.

Female: same as male, but has a black forehead; lacks a red mustache

Juvenile: similar to adults, only duller and browner

Nest: cavity; male and female excavate; 1 brood per year

Eggs: 3–5; white without markings

Incubation: 15–18 days; female incubates during the day, male incubates at night

Fledging: 26–28 days; female and male feed the young

Migration: non-migrator

Food: insects; will come to suet and peanut feeders

Compare: Red-headed Woodpecker (pg. 53) is about half the size and has an all-red head. Look for the bright red crest and exceptionally large size to identify the Pileated Woodpecker.

Stan's Notes: Our largest woodpecker. The common name comes from *pileatus*, which means "wearing a cap," referring to its crest. A relatively shy bird that prefers large tracts of woodland. Drums on hollow branches, chimneys and so forth to announce its territory. Excavates oval holes up to several feet long in tree trunks, looking for insects to eat. Large wood chips lie on the ground by excavated trees. Favorite food is carpenter ants. Feeds regurgitated insects to its young. Young emerge from the nest looking just like the adults.

soaring

SUMMER

Osprey
Pandion haliaetus

Size: 21–24" (53–61 cm); up to 5½-ft. wingspan

Male: Large eagle-like bird with a white chest, belly and head. Dark eye line. Nearly black back. Black "wrist" marks on the wings. Dark bill.

Female: same as male, only slightly larger and has a necklace of brown streaks

Juvenile: similar to adults, with a light tan breast

Nest: platform, on a raised wooden platform, man-made tower or tall dead tree; female and male build; 1 brood per year

Eggs: 2–4; white with brown markings

Incubation: 32–42 days; female and male incubate

Fledging: 48–58 days; male and female feed the young

Migration: complete, to southern states, Mexico, Central and South America

Food: fish

Compare: The juvenile Bald Eagle (pg. 71) is brown with white speckles. The adult Bald Eagle has an all-white head and tail. Look for the white belly and dark eye line to identify the Osprey.

Stan's Notes: The only species in its family, and the only raptor that plunges into water feet first to catch fish. Always near water. Can hover for a few seconds before diving. Carries fish in a head-first position for better aerodynamics. Wings angle back in flight. Often harassed by Bald Eagles for its catch. Gives a high-pitched, whistle-like call, often calling in flight as a warning. Mates have a long-term pair bond. Northern birds may not migrate to the same wintering ground. Was nearly extinct but now doing well.

breeding

winter

Common Loon
Gavia immer

SUMMER
MIGRATION

Size: 28–36" (71–91 cm)

Male: Checkerboard back, black head, white neck-lace. Deep red eyes. Long, pointed black bill. Winter plumage has a gray body and bill.

Female: same as male

Juvenile: similar to winter plumage, but lacks red eyes

Nest: ground, usually at the shoreline; female and male build; 1 brood per year

Eggs: 2; olive-brown, occasionally brown markings

Incubation: 26–31 days; female and male incubate

Fledging: 75–80 days; female and male feed the young

Migration: complete, to southern states, the Gulf Coast and Mexico

Food: fish, aquatic insects, crayfish, salamanders

Compare: The Double-crested Cormorant (pg. 41) has a black chest and gray bill with a hooked tip and yellow at the base. Look for a checkerboard back to identify the Common Loon.

Stan's Notes: Hunts for fish by eyesight and prefers clear, clean lakes. A great swimmer, but its legs are set so far back that it has a hard time walking. "Loon" comes from the Scandinavian term *lom*, meaning "lame," for the awkward way it walks on land. To take off, it faces into the wind and runs on the water while flapping. Its wailing call suggests wild laughter, which led to the phrase "crazy as a loon." Also gives soft hoots. In the water, young ride on the backs of their parents for about 10 days. Adults perform distraction displays to protect the young. Very sensitive to disturbance during nesting and will abandon the nest.

soaring

juvenile

soaring
juvenile

Bald Eagle

Haliaeetus leucocephalus

SUMMER
MIGRATION
WINTER

Size: 31–37" (79–94 cm); up to 7½-ft. wingspan

Male: White head and tail contrast sharply with the dark brown-to-black body and wings. Large, curved yellow bill and yellow feet.

Female: same as male, only larger

Juvenile: dark brown with white speckles and spots on the body and wings, gray bill

Nest: massive platform, usually in a tree; female and male build; 1 brood per year

Eggs: 2–3; off-white without markings

Incubation: 34–36 days; female and male incubate

Fledging: 75–90 days; female and male feed the young

Migration: partial migrator, to southeastern states

Food: fish, carrion, birds (mainly ducks)

Compare: Turkey Vulture (pg. 39) is smaller, has two-toned wings and holds them in a V shape in flight. The Eagle holds its wings straight out.

Stan's Notes: Nearly became extinct due to DDT poisoning and illegal killing. Now making a comeback in North America. Returns to the same nest each year, adding more sticks and enlarging it to huge proportions, at times up to 1,000 pounds (450 kg). In their midair mating ritual, one eagle flips upside down and locks talons with another. Both tumble, then break apart to continue flight. Not uncommon for juveniles to perform this mating ritual even though they have not reached breeding age. Long-term pair bond but will switch mates when not successful at reproducing. Juveniles attain the white head and tail at 4–5 years of age.

female
pg. 105

male

SUMMER

Indigo Bunting
Passerina cyanea

Size: 5½" (14 cm)

Male: Vibrant blue finch-like bird. Dark markings scattered on wings and tail.

Female: light brown bird with faint markings

Juvenile: similar to female

Nest: cup; female builds; 2 broods per year

Eggs: 3–4; pale blue without markings

Incubation: 12–13 days; female incubates

Fledging: 10–11 days; female feeds the young

Migration: complete, to Florida, Mexico, Central and South America

Food: insects, seeds, fruit; will visit seed feeders

Compare: Male Eastern Bluebird (pg. 79) is larger and has a rust-red chest. Look for the bright blue plumage to identify the male Indigo Bunting.

Stan's Notes: Seen along woodland edges and in parks and yards, feeding on insects. Comes to seed feeders early in spring, before insects are plentiful. Usually only the males are noticed. Male often sings from treetops to attract a mate. Female is quiet. Actually a gray bird, without blue pigment in its feathers. Like Blue Jays and other blue birds, sunlight is refracted within the structure of the male's feathers, making them appear blue. Plumage is iridescent in direct sun, duller in shade. Molts in spring to acquire body feathers with gray tips, which quickly wear off, revealing the bright blue plumage. Molts in fall and appears like the female during winter. Migrates at night in flocks of 5–10 birds. Males return before the females and juveniles, often to the nest site of the preceding year. Juveniles move to within a mile of their birth site.

SUMMER

Tree Swallow
Tachycineta bicolor

Size: 5–6" (13–15 cm)

Male: Blue-green in spring, greener in fall. Changes color in direct sunlight. White from chin to belly. Long, pointed wing tips. Notched tail.

Female: similar to male, only duller

Juvenile: gray-brown with a white belly and a grayish breast band

Nest: cavity; female and male line a vacant woodpecker cavity or nest box; 2 broods per year

Eggs: 4–6; white without markings

Incubation: 13–16 days; female incubates

Fledging: 20–24 days; female and male feed the young

Migration: complete, to Mexico and Central America

Food: insects

Compare: The Purple Martin (pg. 81) is much larger and darker. The Barn Swallow (pg. 77) has a rusty belly and a long, deeply forked tail. Look for the white chin, chest and belly and the notched tail to help identify the Tree Swallow.

Stan's Notes: Found at ponds, lakes, rivers and farm fields. Often seen flying back and forth across fields, feeding on insects. Can be attracted to your yard with a nest box. Competes with the Eastern Bluebird for tree cavities and nest boxes. Builds a grass nest within and will travel long distances, looking for dropped feathers for the lining. Watch for it playing, chasing after feathers. Flies with rapid wingbeats, then glides. Gives a series of gurgles and chirps. Chatters when upset or threatened. Eats many nuisance bugs, so good to have around. Families gather in large flocks for migration.

Barn Swallow

Hirundo rustica

SUMMER

Size: 7" (18 cm)

Male: A sleek swallow. Blue-black back, cinnamon belly and reddish-brown chin. White spots on a long, deeply forked tail.

Female: same as male, but has a whitish belly

Juvenile: similar to adults, with a tan belly and chin and a shorter tail

Nest: cup; female and male build; 2 broods per year

Eggs: 4–5; white with brown markings

Incubation: 13–17 days; female incubates

Fledging: 18–23 days; female and male feed the young

Migration: complete, to South America

Food: insects (prefers beetles, wasps, flies)

Compare: Tree Swallow (pg. 75) is white from chin to belly. Purple Martin (pg. 81) is larger and has a dark purple belly. Chimney Swift (pg. 91) has a narrow, pointed tail. Look for the deeply forked tail to help identify the Barn Swallow.

Stan's Notes: Seen in wetlands, farms, suburban yards and parks. Michigan has six swallow species, but this is the only one with a deeply forked tail. Unlike other swallows, it rarely glides in flight. Usually flies low over land or water. Drinks as it flies, skimming water, or will sip water droplets on wet leaves. Bathes while flying through rain or sprinklers. Gives a twittering warble, followed by a mechanical sound. Builds a mud nest with up to 1,000 beak-loads of mud. Nests on barns, houses, under bridges and other sheltered places. Often nests in colonies of 4–6 birds; sometimes nests alone.

male

female

SUMMER

Eastern Bluebird
Sialia sialis

Size: 7" (18 cm)

Male: Sky-blue head, back and tail. Rust-red breast and white belly.

Female: grayer than the male, with a faint rusty breast and faint blue wings and tail

Juvenile: similar to female, but spots on the breast and blue wing markings

Nest: cavity, vacant woodpecker cavity or nest box; female adds a soft lining; 2 broods per year

Eggs: 4–5; pale blue without markings

Incubation: 12–14 days; female incubates

Fledging: 15–18 days; male and female feed the young

Migration: complete, to southern states

Food: insects, fruit; comes to shallow dishes with live or dead mealworms, and to suet feeders

Compare: The male Indigo Bunting (pg. 73) is nearly all blue. The Blue Jay (pg. 83) is much larger and has a crest. Look for the rusty breast to help identify the Eastern Bluebird.

Stan's Notes: Was nearly eliminated from Michigan due to a lack of nest cavities. Thanks to people who installed thousands of nest boxes, bluebirds now thrive. Prefers open habitats, such as farm fields, pastures and roadsides, but also likes forest edges, parks and yards. Easily tamed. Often perches on trees or fence posts and drops to the ground to grab bugs, especially grasshoppers. Makes short flights from tree to tree. Song is a distinctive "churlee chur chur-lee." The rust-red breast is like that of the American Robin, its cousin. The young of the first brood help raise the second brood.

male

female

SUMMER

Purple Martin
Progne subis

Size: 8½" (21.5 cm)

Male: Iridescent bird with a purple-to-black head, back and belly, black wings and a notched black tail.

Female: grayish-purple head and back, darker wings and tail, whitish belly

Juvenile: same as female

Nest: cavity; female and male line the cavity of the house; 1 brood per year

Eggs: 4–5; white without markings

Incubation: 15–18 days; female incubates

Fledging: 26–30 days; male and female feed the young

Migration: complete, to South America

Food: insects

Compare: Usually only seen in groups. The male Purple Martin is the only swallow with a very dark purplish belly.

Stan's Notes: The largest swallow species in North America. Once nested in tree cavities. Now nests almost exclusively in man-made apartment-style houses. The most successful colonies often nest in multiunit nest boxes within 100 feet (30 m) of a human dwelling near a lake. The main diet consists of dragonflies, not mosquitoes, as once thought. Gives a continuous stream of chirps, creaks and rattles, along with a shout-like "churrr" and chortle. Often drinks in flight, skimming water, and bathes in flight, flying through rain. Returns to the same nest site each year. Males arrive before females and yearlings. The young leave to form new colonies. Large colonies gather in fall before migrating to South America.

YEAR-ROUND

Blue Jay
Cyanocitta cristata

Size: 12" (30 cm)

Male: Bright light blue-and-white bird with a black necklace and gray belly. Large crest moves up and down at will. White face, wing bars and tip of tail. Black tail bands.

Female: same as male

Juvenile: same as adult, only duller

Nest: cup; female and male construct; 1–2 broods per year

Eggs: 4–5; green-to-blue with brown markings

Incubation: 16–18 days; female incubates

Fledging: 17–21 days; female and male feed the young

Migration: non-migrator to partial; will move around in winter to find an abundant food source

Food: insects, fruit, carrion, seeds, nuts; visits seed feeders, ground feeders with corn or peanuts

Compare: Belted Kingfisher (pg. 85) has a larger, more ragged crest. The Eastern Bluebird (pg. 79) is much smaller and has a rust-red breast. Look for the large crest to help identify the Blue Jay.

Stan's Notes: A highly intelligent bird, solving problems, gathering food and communicating more than other birds. Loud, noisy and mimics other birds. Known as the alarm of the forest, screaming at intruders. Imitates hawk calls around feeders to scare off other birds. One of the few birds to cache food. Can remember where it hid thousands of nuts. Carries seeds and nuts in a pouch under its tongue (sublingual). Eats bird eggs and young birds in other nests. Feathers lack blue pigment; refracted sunlight casts the blue light.

male

female

Belted Kingfisher
Megaceryle alcyon

SUMMER

Size: 12–14" (30–36 cm)

Male: Blue with a white belly, blue-gray chest band, black wing tips. Ragged crest moves up and down at will. Large head. Long, thick black bill. White spot by the eyes. Red-brown eyes.

Female: same as male, but has rusty flanks and a rusty chest band under a blue-gray band

Juvenile: similar to female

Nest: cavity; female and male excavate in a bank of a river, lake or cliff; 1 brood per year

Eggs: 6–7; white without markings

Incubation: 23–24 days; female and male incubate

Fledging: 23–24 days; female and male feed the young

Migration: complete, to southern states, Mexico, Central and South America

Food: small fish

Compare: The Blue Jay (pg. 83) is lighter blue and has a plain gray chest and belly. Belted Kingfisher is rarely found away from water.

Stan's Notes: Usually found at the bank of a river, lake or large stream. Perches on a branch near water, dives in headfirst to catch a small fish, then returns to the branch to feed. Parents drop dead fish into the water to teach their young to dive. Can't pass bones through its digestive tract; regurgitates bone pellets after meals. Gives a loud call that sounds like a machine gun. Mates know each other by their calls. Digs a tunnel up to 4 feet (1 m) long to a nest chamber. Small white patches on dark wing tips flash during flight.

SUMMER

Chestnut-sided Warbler
Setophaga pensylvanica

Size: 5" (13 cm)

Male: Colorful combination of a bright yellow cap, black mask and white face, with a white chest and belly. Chestnut flanks. Gray wings with two yellow wing bars. White undertail.

Female: similar to male, with duller brown flanks

Juvenile: similar to female, with a lime-green head and back, white eye-ring and bright yellow wing bars; lacks chestnut sides

Nest: cup; female builds; 1 brood per year

Eggs: 3–5; white with brown markings

Incubation: 12–13 days; female incubates

Fledging: 10–12 days; female and male feed the young

Migration: complete, to Central America

Food: insects, berries

Compare: The Yellow-rumped Warbler (pg. 201) has yellow patches on its sides and rump. Yellow Warbler (pg. 293) is nearly all yellow. Look for the yellow cap and chestnut flanks to help identify the Chestnut-sided Warbler.

Stan's Notes: A very attractive warbler, named for the chestnut patches on its sides. Prefers an open, young aspen forest. During migration, often attracted to backyard water gardens that have a small trickling stream. Look for it in spring, hopping high up in trees while it hunts for insects. Usually you will only get a glimpse of this fast-moving bird. Holds tail in an uplifted position, showing the white undertail. Not uncommon for it to approach people near its nest in defense of the site.

Brown Creeper
Certhia americana

YEAR-ROUND

Size: 5" (13 cm)

Male: Small, thin, nearly camouflaged brown bird. White from chin to belly. White eyebrows. Dark eyes and a thin, curved bill. Tail is long and stiff.

Female: same as male

Juvenile: same as adult

Nest: cup; female constructs; 1 brood per year

Eggs: 5–6; white with tiny brown markings

Incubation: 14–17 days; female incubates, male feeds the female during incubation

Fledging: 13–16 days; female and male feed the young

Migration: partial to non-migrator

Food: insects, nuts, seeds

Compare: Red-breasted Nuthatch (pg. 195) and White-breasted Nuthatch (pg. 199) climb down tree trunks, not up. To spot a Brown Creeper, look for a small brown bird with a white belly creeping up trees.

Stan's Notes: A forest bird, commonly found in wooded habitats. Will fly from the top of one tree trunk to the bottom of another, then work its way to the top, looking for caterpillars, spider eggs and more. Its long tail has tiny spines underneath, which help it cling to trees. Uses its camouflage coloring to hide in plain sight. Spreads out flat on a branch or trunk and won't move. Often builds its nest behind the loose bark of a dead or dying tree. Young follow their parents around, creeping up trees soon after fledging.

Chimney Swift
Chaetura pelagica

SUMMER

Size: 5" (13 cm)

Male: Nondescript, cigar-shaped bird, usually only seen in flight. Long, thin brown body. Pointed tail and head. Long, swept-back wings, longer than the body.

Female: same as male

Juvenile: same as adult

Nest: half cup; female and male construct; 1 brood per year

Eggs: 4–5; white without markings

Incubation: 19–21 days; female and male incubate

Fledging: 28–30 days; female and male feed the young

Migration: complete, to South America

Food: insects caught in midair

Compare: Purple Martin (pg. 81) is much larger and darker. Barn Swallow (pg. 77) has a deeply forked tail. Tree Swallow (pg. 75) has a white belly and blue-green back. Look for the cigar shape to identify the Chimney Swift in flight.

Stan's Notes: One of the fastest fliers in the bird world. Spends all day flying, rarely perching. Flies in groups, feeding on insects flying 100 feet (30 m) or higher up in the air. Often called Flying Cigar due to its body shape, which is pointed at both ends. Drinks and bathes during flight, skimming water. Gives a unique in-flight twittering call, often heard before the bird is seen. Hundreds roost in large chimneys, giving it the common name. Builds its nest with tiny twigs, cementing it with saliva and attaching it to the inside of a chimney or a hollow tree. Usually only one nest per chimney.

Chipping Sparrow
Spizella passerina

SUMMER

Size: 5" (13 cm)

Male: Small gray-brown sparrow with a clear gray chest, white eyebrows, thin black eye line and rusty crown. Thin gray-black bill. Two faint wing bars.

Female: same as male

Juvenile: similar to adult, with streaking on the chest; lacks a rusty crown

Nest: cup; female builds; 2 broods per year

Eggs: 3–5; blue-green with brown markings

Incubation: 11–14 days; female incubates

Fledging: 10–12 days; female and male feed the young

Migration: complete, to southern states, Mexico and Central America

Food: insects, seeds; will come to ground feeders

Compare: American Tree Sparrow (pg. 111) has gray eyebrows and a rusty eye line. The Song Sparrow (pg. 109), Fox Sparrow (pg. 121) and female House Finch (pg. 99) have heavily streaked chests. Look for the rusty crown and black eye line to identify the Chipping Sparrow.

Stan's Notes: A common garden or yard bird, often seen feeding on dropped seeds beneath feeders. Gathers in large family groups to feed in preparation for migration. Migrates at night in flocks of 20–30 birds. The common name comes from the male's fast "chip" call. Often just called Chippy. Builds nest low in dense shrubs and almost always lines it with animal hair. Comfortable with people, allowing you to approach closely before it flies away.

male

Hoary Redpoll

female

WINTER

Common Redpoll
Acanthis flammea

Size: 5" (13 cm)

Male: A sparrow-like bird with a bright red crown and raspberry-red on the chest. Black spot on the chin. Heavily streaked back.

Female: similar to male, but lacks raspberry-red on the chest

Juvenile: browner than adults, with dark streaking on the chest; lacks a red crown

Nest: cup; female builds; 1 brood (occasionally 2) per year

Eggs: 4–5; pale green with purple markings

Incubation: 10–11 days; female incubates

Fledging: 11–12 days; female and male feed the young

Migration: irruptive; moves into Michigan from the far reaches of Canada in some winters

Food: seeds, insects; will come to seed feeders

Compare: Pine Siskin (pg. 97) has yellow wing bars and a streaked chest. Look for the bright red crown and black spot under the bill to help identify the Common Redpoll.

Stan's Notes: Moves from location to location, wheeling around in the sky before landing at feeders. Visits feeders in small to large flocks. Flocks of up 100 birds are not uncommon but not seen at all in some winters. Bathes in open water or snow during winter. Like the Black-capped Chickadee, it can be tamed and hand fed. Gives a zipping call in long strings that last 30 seconds or longer. Also gives a nasal, rising whistle. Hoary Redpoll (see inset) is paler with less streaking on the flanks and a pink wash on the chest.

95

Pine Siskin
Spinus pinus

YEAR-ROUND WINTER

Size: 5" (13 cm)

Male: Small brown finch with heavy streaking on the back, breast and belly. Yellow wing bars. Yellow at the base of tail. Thin bill.

Female: similar to male, with less yellow

Juvenile: similar to adult, with a light yellow tinge over the breast and chin

Nest: cup; female builds; 2 broods

Eggs: 3–4; greenish-blue with brown markings

Incubation: 12–13 days; female incubates

Fledging: 14–15 days; female and male feed the young

Migration: irruptive; moves around Michigan and the U.S. in search of food

Food: seeds, insects; will come to seed feeders

Compare: Female Purple Finch (pg. 115) has white eyebrows. The female House Finch (pg. 99) lacks any yellow. The female American Goldfinch (pg. 287) has white wing bars. Look for the yellow wing bars to identify the Pine Siskin.

Stan's Notes: Usually considered a winter finch. Conspicuous in some winters, rare in others. Seen in flocks of up to 20 birds, often with other finch species. Gathers in flocks and moves around, visiting feeders. Will come to thistle feeders. Gives a series of high-pitched, wheezy calls. Also gives a wheezing twitter. Breeds in small groups. Builds nest toward the end of coniferous branches, where needles are dense, helping to conceal. Nests are often only a few feet apart. Male feeds the female during incubation. Juveniles lose the yellow tint by late summer of their first year.

male
pg. 261

female

House Finch
Haemorhous mexicanus

YEAR-ROUND

Size: 5" (13 cm)

Female: Plain brown bird with heavy streaking on a white chest.

Male: red-to-orange face, throat, chest and rump, brown cap, brown marking behind the eyes, streaked belly and wings

Juvenile: similar to female

Nest: cup, occasionally in a cavity, female builds; 2 broods per year

Eggs: 4–5; pale blue, lightly marked

Incubation: 12–14 days; female incubates

Fledging: 15–19 days; female and male feed the young

Migration: non-migrator to partial; will move around to find food

Food: seeds, fruit, leaf buds; visits seed feeders and feeders that offer grape jelly

Compare: The female Purple Finch (pg. 115) has bold white eyebrows. Pine Siskin (pg. 97) has yellow wing bars and a smaller bill. Female American Goldfinch (pg. 287) has a clear chest. Look for the heavily streaked chest to help identify the female House Finch.

Stan's Notes: Can be a common bird at your feeders. A very social bird, visiting feeders in small flocks. Likes to nest in hanging flower baskets. Male sings a loud, cheerful warbling song. It was originally introduced to Long Island, New York, from the western U.S. in the 1940s. Now found throughout the country. Suffers from a disease that causes the eyes to crust, resulting in blindness and death.

SUMMER

House Wren
Troglodytes aedon

Size: 5" (13 cm)

Male: All-brown bird with lighter brown markings on the wings and tail. Slightly curved brown bill. Often holds tail upward.

Female: same as male

Juvenile: same as adult

Nest: cavity; female and male line just about any nest cavity; 2 broods per year

Eggs: 4–6; tan with brown markings

Incubation: 10–13 days; female and male incubate

Fledging: 12–15 days; female and male feed the young

Migration: complete, to southern states and Mexico

Food: insects, spiders, snails

Compare: The Carolina Wren (pg. 103) and all other species of wrens have eyebrows. The slightly curved bill and the upward position of the tail differentiates the House Wren from sparrows.

Stan's Notes: A prolific songster. During the mating season, sings from dawn to dusk. Seen in brushy yards, parks, woodlands and along forest edges. Easily attracted to a nest box. In spring, the male chooses several prospective nesting cavities and places a few small twigs in each. The female inspects all of them and finishes constructing the nest in the cavity of her choice. She fills the cavity with short twigs, and then lines a small depression at the back with pine needles and grass. She often has trouble fitting longer twigs through the entrance hole and tries many different directions and approaches until she is successful.

YEAR-ROUND

Carolina Wren
Thryothorus ludovicianus

Size: 5½" (14 cm)

Male: Warm rust-brown head and back with an orange-yellow chest and belly. White throat and a prominent white eye stripe. A short, stubby tail, often cocked up.

Female: same as male

Juvenile: same as adult

Nest: cavity; female and male build; 2 broods per year, sometimes 3

Eggs: 4–6; white, sometimes pink or creamy, with brown markings

Incubation: 12–14 days; female incubates

Fledging: 12–14 days; female and male feed young

Migration: non-migrator; moves around to find food

Food: insects, fruit, few seeds; visits suet feeders

Compare: Similar to the House Wren (pg. 101), but Carolina Wren is lighter brown and has a prominent white eye stripe.

Stan's Notes: The Carolina Wren has a long-term pair bond. Mated pairs stay together all year long in their permanent territory. Sings year-round. Male is known to sing up to 40 different song types, singing one song repeatedly before switching to another. Female also sings, resulting in duets. The male often takes over feeding the first brood while the female renests. Nests in birdhouses and in unusual places like mailboxes, bumpers or broken taillights of vehicles, or nearly any other cavity. Found in brushy yards or woodlands. Can be attracted to feeders with mealworms.

female

male
pg. 73

Indigo Bunting
Passerina cyanea

SUMMER

Size: 5½" (14 cm)

Female: A light brown finch-like bird. Faint streaking on a light tan chest. Wings have a very faint blue cast and indistinct wing bars.

Male: vibrant blue with scattered dark markings on wings and tail

Juvenile: similar to female

Nest: cup; female builds; 2 broods per year

Eggs: 3–4; pale blue without markings

Incubation: 12–13 days; female incubates

Fledging: 10–11 days; female feeds the young

Migration: complete, to Florida, Mexico, Central and South America

Food: insects, seeds, fruit; will visit seed feeders

Compare: Female Purple Finch (pg. 115) has white eyebrows and heavy streaking on the chest. Female House Finch (pg. 99) has a heavily streaked chest. Female American Goldfinch (pg. 287) has white wing bars. Look for the faint blue cast on the wings to help identify the female Indigo Bunting.

Stan's Notes: Seen along woodland edges and in parks and yards, feeding on insects. Comes to seed feeders early in spring, before insects are plentiful. Secretive, plain and quiet, usually only the males are noticed. Male often sings from treetops to attract a mate. Migrates at night in flocks of 5–10 birds. Males return before the females and juveniles, often to the nest site of the preceding year. Juveniles move to within a mile of their birth site.

male
pg. 203

female

Dark-eyed Junco
Junco hyemalis

Size: 5½" (14 cm)

Female: A plump, dark-eyed bird with a tan-to-brown chest, head and back. White belly. Ivory-to-pink bill. White outer tail feathers appear like a white V in flight.

Male: round bird with gray plumage

Juvenile: similar to female, with streaking on the breast and head

Nest: cup; female and male build; 2 broods per year

Eggs: 3–5; white with reddish-brown markings

Incubation: 12–13 days; female incubates

Fledging: 10–13 days; male and female feed the young

Migration: complete, to most of Michigan and across the U.S.

Food: seeds, insects; visits ground and seed feeders

Compare: Rarely confused with any other bird. Look for an ivory-to-pink bill and small flocks feeding beneath seed feeders to help identify the female Dark-eyed Junco.

Stan's Notes: One of the most common winter birds in the state. Migrates from Canada and northern parts of Michigan to areas farther south. Adheres to a rigid social hierarchy, with dominant birds chasing the less-dominant birds. Look for the white outer tail feathers flashing in flight. Often seen in small flocks on the ground, where it uses its feet to simultaneously "double-scratch" to expose seeds and insects. Eats many weed seeds. Nests in a wide variety of wooded habitats. Several subspecies of Dark-eyed Junco were previously considered to be separate species.

Song Sparrow
Melospiza melodia

YEAR-ROUND
SUMMER

Size: 5–6" (13–15 cm)

Male: A common brown sparrow with heavy dark streaking on the breast coalescing into a central dark spot.

Female: same as male

Juvenile: similar to adult, with a finely streaked chest; lacks a central dark spot

Nest: cup; female builds; 2 broods per year

Eggs: 3–4; blue-to-green with red-brown markings

Incubation: 12–14 days; female incubates

Fledging: 9–12 days; female and male feed the young

Migration: complete, to southern states; non-migrator in southern parts of the L.P.

Food: insects, seeds; only rarely comes to ground feeders with seeds

Compare: Similar to other brown sparrows. Look for the heavily streaked chest with a central dark spot to help identify the Song Sparrow.

Stan's Notes: There are many subspecies of this bird, but the dark spot in the center of the chest appears in every variety. A constant songster, repeating its loud, clear song every few minutes. The song varies from region to region but has the same basic structure. Sings from thick shrubs to defend a small territory, beginning with three notes and finishing with a trill. A ground feeder, look for it to "double-scratch" with both feet at the same time to expose seeds. When the female builds a new nest for the second brood, the male often feeds the first brood. Unlike many other sparrow species, Song Sparrows rarely flock together. A common host of cowbirds.

WINTER

American Tree Sparrow
Spizelloides arborea

Size: 6" (15 cm)

Male: Brown bird with a tan chest and rusty crown and eye line. Gray eyebrows. Dark spot in the center of chest. Dark upper bill, yellow lower bill. Two white wing bars.

Female: same as male

Juvenile: streaked chest often obscures the central dark spot; lacks a rusty crown

Nest: cup; female builds; 1 brood per year

Eggs: 3–5; greenish-white with brown markings

Incubation: 12–13 days; female incubates

Fledging: 8–10 days; female and male feed the young

Migration: complete, to Michigan and most U.S. states

Food: insects, seeds; visits seed feeders

Compare: The Chipping Sparrow (pg. 93) has white eyebrows and a black eye line. Song Sparrow (pg. 109) has a heavily streaked chest. Look for a dark spot on the chest and a two-toned bill to identify the American Tree Sparrow.

Stan's Notes: A regular feeder visitor in Michigan during winter. Seen during migration in flocks of 2–200 birds. Found in open fields, woodlands and suburban backyards. Occasionally called Winter Chippy because it looks like the Chipping Sparrow. Gives a series of high-pitched, sweet-sounding whistles. Nests in Canada and Alaska. The species name *arborea* means "tree," but it doesn't nest in trees. Nests on the ground in a clump of grass. The name "Tree" refers to its habitat. "American" refers to its natural range.

House Sparrow
Passer domesticus

YEAR-ROUND

Size: 6" (15 cm)

Male: Brown back with a gray belly and cap. Large black patch extending from the throat to the chest (bib). One white wing bar.

Female: slightly smaller than the male, light brown with light eyebrows; lacks a bib and white wing bar

Juvenile: similar to female

Nest: cavity; female and male build a domed cup nest within; 2–3 broods per year

Eggs: 4–6; white with brown markings

Incubation: 10–12 days; female incubates

Fledging: 14–17 days; female and male feed the young

Migration: non-migrator; moves around to find food

Food: seeds, insects, fruit; comes to seed feeders

Compare: The American Tree Sparrow (pg. 111) and the Chipping Sparrow (pg. 93) have a rusty crown. Look for the black bib to identify the male House Sparrow and the clear breast to help identify the female.

Stan's Notes: One of the first birdsongs heard in cities in spring. A familiar city bird, nearly always in small flocks. Also found on farms. Introduced from Europe in 1850 to Central Park in New York. Now seen throughout North America. Related to Old World sparrows; not a relative of any sparrows in the U.S. An aggressive bird that will kill young birds in order to take over the nest cavity. Uses dried grass, small scraps of plastic, paper and other materials to build an oversized domed nest in the cavity.

male
pg. 263

female

Purple Finch
Haemorhous purpureus

Size:	6" (15 cm)
Female:	Plain brown bird with heavy streaking on the chest, bold white eyebrows and a large bill.
Male:	raspberry-red head, cap, breast, back and rump, brownish wings and tail
Juvenile:	same as female
Nest:	cup; female and male build; 1 brood per year
Eggs:	4–5; greenish-blue with brown markings
Incubation:	12–13 days; female incubates
Fledging:	13–14 days; female and male feed the young
Migration:	irruptive; moves around in winter to find food
Food:	seeds, insects, fruit; comes to seed feeders
Compare:	Female House Finch (pg. 99) lacks eyebrows. Pine Siskin (pg. 97) has yellow wing bars. Female American Goldfinch (pg. 287) has a clear chest. Look for bold white eyebrows to identify the female Purple Finch.

YEAR-ROUND
WINTER

Stan's Notes: Found year-round in the northern half of Michigan and during winter in the southern half of the L.P. An irruptive migrator, more common in some parts of the state, but not always seen every winter. Travels in flocks of up to 50 birds. Visits seed feeders along with House Finches, which makes it hard to tell them apart. Ash tree seeds are an important source of food; feeds mainly on seeds. Found in coniferous forests, mixed woods, woodland edges and suburban backyards. Flies in the typical undulating, up-and-down pattern of finches. Sings a rich, loud song. Gives a distinctive "tic" note only in flight. The male is not purple. The Latin species name *purpureus* means "purple" or other reddish colors.

white-striped

tan-striped

White-throated Sparrow
Zonotrichia albicollis

YEAR-ROUND
SUMMER
WINTER

Size: 6–7" (15–18 cm)

Male: Brown sparrow with a gray or tan chest and belly, and a white or tan throat patch and eyebrows. Bold striping on the head. Small yellow spot by each eye (lore).

Female: same as male

Juvenile: similar to adult, with a heavily streaked chest and gray throat and eyebrows

Nest: cup; female builds; 1 brood per year

Eggs: 4–6; green-to-blue or cream-white with red-brown markings

Incubation: 11–14 days; female incubates

Fledging: 10–12 days; female and male feed the young

Migration: complete, to the southern half of the L.P., southern states and Mexico

Food: insects, seeds, fruit; visits ground feeders

Compare: White-crowned Sparrow (pg. 119) lacks the throat patch and yellow lores of the White-throated Sparrow.

Stan's Notes: Two color variations (polymorphic): white-striped and tan-striped. Studies indicate that the white-striped adults tend to mate with the tan-striped birds. It's not clear why. Known for its wonderful song. Sings all year and can even be heard at night. White- and tan-striped males and white-striped females sing, but tan-striped females do not. Builds nest on the ground under small trees in bogs and coniferous forests. Often associated with other sparrows in winter. Feeds on the ground under feeders. Immature and first-year females tend to winter farther south than the adults.

juvenile

White-crowned Sparrow
Zonotrichia leucophrys

MIGRATION

Size:	6½–7½" (16.5–19 cm)
Male:	Brown with a gray chest and black-and-white striped crown. Small, thin pink bill.
Female:	same as male
Juvenile:	similar to adult, with black-and-brown stripes on the head
Nest:	cup; female builds; 2 broods per year
Eggs:	3–5; greenish-to-bluish-to-whitish with red-brown markings
Incubation:	11–14 days; female incubates
Fledging:	8–12 days; male and female feed the young
Migration:	complete, to southern states and Mexico
Food:	insects, seeds, berries; visits ground feeders
Compare:	The White-throated Sparrow (pg. 117) has a throat patch and a small yellow spot by each eye (lore). The Song Sparrow (pg. 109) has a streaked chest. Look for the striped crown to help identify the White-crowned Sparrow.

Stan's Notes: Often in groups of up to 20 birds during migration, when it can be seen visiting ground feeders and feeding beneath seed feeders. A ground feeder that will "double-scratch" backward with both feet simultaneously to find seeds. Prefers scrubby areas, woodland edges and open or grassy habitats. The males are prolific songsters, singing in late winter while migrating northward. Males arrive at the breeding grounds before the females and sing from perches to establish territory. Males take most of the responsibility to raise the young while females start their second broods. Only 9–12 days separate the broods. Nests in Canada and Alaska.

MIGRATION

Fox Sparrow
Passerella iliaca

Size: 7" (18 cm)

Male: A plump, rust-red sparrow. Heavily streaked rusty breast and solid rust tail. Head and back are mottled with gray.

Female: same as male

Juvenile: same as adult

Nest: cup; female builds; 2 broods per year

Eggs: 2–4; pale green with reddish markings

Incubation: 12–14 days; female incubates

Fledging: 10–11 days; female and male feed the young

Migration: complete, to southern states

Food: seeds, insects; comes to ground feeders

Compare: The Brown Thrasher (pg. 147) is much larger, slimmer and has a long, curved bill. The Fox Sparrow's rust-red plumage differentiates it from all other sparrows.

Stan's Notes: One of the largest sparrows. Often alone or in small groups. Found in shrubby areas, open fields and backyards. Comes to ground feeders and seen underneath seed feeders during migration, searching for seeds and insects. Like a chicken, it will "double-scratch" with both feet at the same time to look for food. Gives a series of rich notes lasting 2–3 seconds, usually singing from a perch hidden in a shrub. The common name "Sparrow" comes from the Anglo-Saxon word *spearwa*, meaning "flutterer," as applies to any small bird. "Fox" refers to its rusty color. Appears in several color variations, depending on the part of the country. Nests on the ground in brush and along forest edges in Canada and Alaska.

female

male

Horned Lark
Eremophila alpestris

YEAR-ROUND
SUMMER
MIGRATION

Size: 7–8" (18–20 cm)

Male: A tan-to-brown bird with black markings on the face. Black necklace and bill. Pale yellow chin. Two tiny feather "horns" on the top of head, sometimes hard to see. Dark tail with white outer tail feathers, noticeable in flight.

Female: duller than the male; less noticeable "horns"

Juvenile: lacks a yellow chin and black markings; does not form "horns" until the second year

Nest: ground; female builds; 2–3 broods per year

Eggs: 3–4; gray with brown markings

Incubation: 11–12 days; female incubates

Fledging: 9–12 days; female and male feed the young

Migration: complete, to southern parts of the L.P. and southern states

Food: seeds, insects

Compare: Eastern Meadowlark (pg. 303) has a yellow breast and belly. Look for the black markings by the eyes and the black necklace.

Stan's Notes: The only true lark native to North America. A bird of open ground. Common in rural areas, often seen in large flocks. The population increased in North America over the past century as more land was cleared for farming. Male performs a fluttering courtship flight high in the air while singing a high-pitched song. Female performs a fluttering distraction display when the nest is disturbed. Starts breeding early in the year. Able to renest about a week after the brood fledges. Moves around in winter to find food. "Lark" comes from the Middle English word *laverock*, or "a lark."

male
pg. 47

female

SUMMER

Rose-breasted Grosbeak
Pheucticus ludovicianus

Size:	7–8" (18–20 cm)
Female:	Plump and heavily streaked. Large, obvious white eyebrows. Large ivory bill. Orange-to-yellow wing linings.
Male:	black-and-white with a triangular rose patch in the center of chest, rose-red wing linings
Juvenile:	similar to female
Nest:	cup; female and male construct; 1–2 broods per year
Eggs:	3–5; blue-green with brown markings
Incubation:	13–14 days; female and male incubate
Fledging:	9–12 days; female and male feed the young
Migration:	complete, to Mexico, Central America and South America
Food:	insects, seeds, fruit; comes to seed feeders
Compare:	Looks like a large finch with bold white eyebrows and heavy streaking. Female Purple Finch (pg. 115) has smaller eyebrows. Female House Finch (pg. 99) lacks eyebrows.

Stan's Notes: Seen in small groups. Prefers a mature deciduous forest for nesting. Both sexes sing, but the male sings much louder and clearer. Sings a rich, robin-like song with a chip note in the tune. "Grosbeak" refers to the thick, strong bill, which is used to crush seeds. Males arrive at the breeding grounds a few days before females. Several males will visit seed feeders together in spring. When females arrive, males become territorial and reduce the feeder visits. After fledging, young grosbeaks visit feeders with adults. Makes short flights from tree to tree with rapid wingbeats.

male
pg. 23

Eastern Towhee
Pipilo erythrophthalmus

SUMMER

Size:	7–8" (18–20 cm)
Female:	A mostly light brown bird. Rusty red-brown sides and a white belly. Long brown tail with a white tip. Short, stout, pointed bill and rich red eyes. White wing patches flash in flight.
Male:	similar to female, but black instead of brown
Juvenile:	light brown with heavily streaked head, chest and belly, a long dark tail with a white tip
Nest:	cup; female builds; 2 broods per year
Eggs:	3–4; cream-white with brown markings
Incubation:	12–13 days; female incubates
Fledging:	10–12 days; male and female feed young
Migration:	complete, to southern states, Mexico, Central and South America
Food:	insects, seeds, fruit; visits ground feeders
Compare:	Smaller than the American Robin (pg. 219), which has a red breast and lacks the white belly. The female Rose-breasted Grosbeak (pg. 125) has a heavily streaked breast and obvious white eyebrows.

Stan's Notes: Named for its distinctive "tow-hee" call, given by both sexes. Known mostly for its other characteristic call, which sounds like "drink-your-tea!" Will hop backward with both feet (bilateral scratching), raking up leaf litter to locate insects and seeds. The female does the brooding. Male feeds the young most of the time. In southern coastal states, some individuals have red eyes; others have white eyes. Only the red-eyed variety is seen in Michigan.

male
pg. 25

female

SUMMER

Brown-headed Cowbird
Molothrus ater

Size: 7½" (19 cm)

Female: Dull brown bird with no obvious markings. Pointed, sharp gray bill. Dark eyes.

Male: glossy black with a chocolate-brown head

Juvenile: similar to female, but dull gray plumage with a streaked chest

Nest: no nest; lays eggs in the nests of other birds

Eggs: 5–7; white with brown markings

Incubation: 10–13 days; host birds incubate the eggs

Fledging: 10–11 days; host birds feed the young

Migration: complete, to southern states

Food: insects, seeds; will come to seed feeders

Compare: Female Red-winged Blackbird (pg. 137) has white eyebrows and heavy streaking. Female Indigo Bunting (pg. 105) has faint blue on its wings. Look for the pointed gray bill to help identify the female Brown-headed Cowbird.

Stan's Notes: Cowbirds are members of the blackbird family. Known as brood parasites, Brown-headed Cowbirds are the only parasitic birds in Michigan. Brood parasites lay their eggs in the nests of other birds, leaving the host birds to raise their young. Cowbirds are known to have laid their eggs in the nests of over 200 species of birds. While some birds reject cowbird eggs, most incubate them and raise the young, even to the exclusion of their own. Look for warblers and other birds feeding young birds twice their own size. Named "Cowbird" for its habit of following bison and cattle herds to feed on insects flushed up by the animals.

1 year
old

Bohemian
Waxwing

YEAR-ROUND
SUMMER

Cedar Waxwing
Bombycilla cedrorum

Size: 7½" (19 cm)

Male: A sleek-looking gray-to-brown bird. Pointed crest, bandit-like mask and light yellow belly. Bold yellow tip of tail. Red wing tips look like they were dipped in red wax.

Female: same as male

Juvenile: grayish with a heavily streaked breast; lacks a sleek look, black mask and red wing tips

Nest: cup; female and male construct; 1 brood per year, occasionally 2

Eggs: 4–6; pale blue with brown markings

Incubation: 10–12 days; female incubates

Fledging: 14–18 days; female and male feed the young

Migration: partial migrator, moves around to find food

Food: cedar cones, fruit, seeds, insects

Compare: The female Northern Cardinal (pg. 135) has a large red bill. Bohemian Waxwing (see inset), is larger, less common and has white on its wings and rust under its tail. Look for the red wing tips to help identify the Cedar Waxwing.

Stan's Notes: The name is derived from its red wax-like wing tips and preference for the small, berry-like cones of the cedar. Seen in flocks, moving around from area to area, looking for berries. Feeds on insects during summer, before berries are abundant. Wanders during winter, searching for food supplies. Spends most of its time at the top of tall trees. Listen for the high-pitched "sreee" whistling sound it constantly makes while perched or in flight. Obtains the mask after the first year and red wing tips after the second year.

winter

breeding

Spotted Sandpiper
Actitis macularius

SUMMER

Size: 8" (20 cm)

Male: Olive-brown back with black spots on a white chest and belly. White line over eyes. Long, dull yellow legs. Long bill. Winter plumage lacks spots on the chest and belly.

Female: same as male

Juvenile: similar to winter plumage, with a darker bill

Nest: ground; male builds; 2 broods per year

Eggs: 3–4; brownish with brown markings

Incubation: 20–24 days; male incubates

Fledging: 17–21 days; male feeds the young

Migration: complete, to southern states, Mexico, Central and South America

Food: aquatic insects

Compare: Greater Yellowlegs (pg. 157) is much larger. Killdeer (pg. 145) has two black neck bands. Look for the black spots on the chest and belly and the bobbing tail to help identify the breeding Spotted Sandpiper.

Stan's Notes: Seen along the shorelines of large ponds, lakes and rivers. One of the few shorebirds that will dive underwater when pursued. Able to fly straight up out of the water. Holds wings in a cup-like arc in flight, rarely lifting them above a horizontal plane. Walks as if delicately balanced. When standing, constantly bobs its tail. Gives a rapid series of "weet-weet-weet" calls when frightened and flying away. Female mates with multiple males and lays eggs in up to five nests. Male does all of the nest building, incubating and childcare without any help from the female.

male
pg. 267

female

juvenile

Northern Cardinal
Cardinalis cardinalis

YEAR-ROUND

Size: 8–9" (20–23 cm)

Female: Buff-brown with a black mask, large reddish bill, and red tinges on the crest and wings.

Male: red with a large crest and bill, and black mask extending from the face to the throat

Juvenile: same as female, but with a blackish-gray bill

Nest: cup; female builds; 2–3 broods per year

Eggs: 3–4; bluish-white with brown markings

Incubation: 12–13 days; female and male incubate

Fledging: 9–10 days; female and male feed the young

Migration: non-migrator

Food: seeds, insects, fruit; comes to seed feeders

Compare: The Cedar Waxwing (pg. 131) has a small dark bill. The juvenile Northern Cardinal (see inset) looks like the adult female Cardinal, but the juvenile has a dark bill. Look for the reddish bill to identify the female Northern Cardinal.

Stan's Notes: A familiar backyard bird. Seen in a variety of habitats, including parks. Usually likes thick vegetation. One of the few species in which both females and males sing. Can be heard all year. Listen for its "whata-cheer-cheer-cheer" territorial call in spring. Watch for a male feeding a female during courtship. The male also feeds the young of the first brood while the female builds a second nest. Territorial in spring, fighting its own reflection in a window or other reflective surface. Non-territorial in winter, gathering in small flocks of up to 20 birds. Makes short flights from cover to cover, often landing on the ground. *Cardinalis* denotes importance, as represented by the red priestly garments of Catholic cardinals.

male
pg. 29

female

SUMMER

Red-winged Blackbird
Agelaius phoeniceus

Size: 8½" (21.5 cm)

Female: Heavily streaked brown bird with a pointed brown bill and white eyebrows.

Male: jet-black bird with red-and-yellow shoulder patches (epaulets) and a pointed black bill

Juvenile: same as female

Nest: cup; female builds; 2–3 broods per year

Eggs: 3–4; bluish-green with brown markings

Incubation: 10–12 days; female incubates

Fledging: 11–14 days; female and male feed the young

Migration: complete, to southern states, Mexico and Central America

Food: seeds, insects; visits seed and suet feeders

Compare: Female Rose-breasted Grosbeak (pg. 125) is more plump and has a thicker bill. Female Brown-headed Cowbird (pg. 129) lacks any streaks. Look for white eyebrows and heavy streaking to identify the female Red-winged.

Stan's Notes: One of the most widespread and numerous birds in Michigan. Found around marshes, wetlands, lakes and rivers. It is a sure sign of spring when these birds return home. Flocks with as many as 10,000 birds have been reported. Males arrive before the females and sing to defend their territory. The male repeats his call from the top of a cattail while showing off his red-and-yellow shoulder patches. The female chooses a mate and often builds her nest over shallow water in a thick stand of cattails. The male can be aggressive when defending the nest. Feeds mostly on seeds in spring and fall, and insects throughout the summer.

female

male

SUMMER

Common Nighthawk
Chordeiles minor

Size: 9" (23 cm)

Male: Camouflaged brown-and-white bird with a white chin. Distinctive white band across the wings and tail, seen only in flight.

Female: similar to male, with a tan chin; lacks a white tail band

Juvenile: similar to female

Nest: no nest; lays eggs on the ground, usually on rocks or a rooftop; 1 brood per year

Eggs: 2; cream with lavender markings

Incubation: 19–20 days; female and male incubate

Fledging: 20–21 days; female and male feed the young

Migration: complete, to South America

Food: insects caught in the air

Compare: The Chimney Swift (pg. 91) is much smaller. Look for the obvious white band on the wings and characteristic flap-flap-flap-glide pattern to help identify the Common Nighthawk.

Stan's Notes: Usually only seen in flight at dusk or after sunset but not uncommon to see it sleeping on a branch during the day. A prolific insect eater and very noisy in flight, repeating a "peenting" call. Alternates slow wingbeats with bursts of quick wingbeats. In cities, prefers to nest on flat rooftops with gravel. City populations are on the decline as gravel rooftops are converted to other styles. In spring, the male performs a showy mating ritual consisting of a steep diving flight ending with a loud popping noise. One of the first birds to migrate in fall. Seen in large flocks, all heading south.

in flight

male

juvenile

female

in-flight
juvenile

YEAR-ROUND
SUMMER

American Kestrel
Falco sparverius

Size: 9–11" (23–28 cm); up to 2-ft. wingspan

Male: Rust-brown back and tail. White breast with dark spots. Two vertical black lines on a white face. Blue-gray wings. Wide black band with a white edge on the tip of a rusty tail.

Female: similar to male, only slightly larger, with rust-brown wings and dark bands on the tail

Juvenile: same as adult of the same sex

Nest: cavity; doesn't build a nest; 1 brood per year

Eggs: 4–5; white with brown markings

Incubation: 29–31 days; male and female incubate

Fledging: 30–31 days; female and male feed the young

Migration: complete, to southern states, Mexico and Central America, some do not migrate

Food: insects, small mammals and birds, reptiles

Compare: The Peregrine Falcon (pg. 233) is much larger and has a dark "hood" and mustache mark. Look for two vertical black stripes on the face to help identify the Kestrel. No other small bird of prey has a rusty back and tail.

Stan's Notes: An unusual raptor because the sexes look different (dimorphic). A falcon that was once called Sparrow Hawk due to its small size. Hovers near roads, then dives for prey. Watch for it to pump its tail after landing on a perch. Perches nearly upright. Eats many grasshoppers. Adapts quickly to a wooden nest box. Can be extremely vocal, giving a loud series of high-pitched calls. Able to see ultraviolet (UV) light, enabling it to find mice and other prey by their urine, which glows bright yellow in UV light.

Lesser Yellowlegs

Tringa flavipes

MIGRATION

Size: 10–12" (25–30 cm)

Male: A typical sandpiper-type bird with a brown back and wings, and a streaked white chest. Thin, straight black bill. Long yellow legs.

Female: same as male

Juvenile: same as adult

Nest: ground; female builds; 1 brood per year

Eggs: 3–4; yellowish with brown markings

Incubation: 22–23 days; male and female incubate

Fledging: 18–20 days; male and female lead the young to food

Migration: complete, to southern coastal states, Mexico, Central and South America

Food: aquatic insects, tiny fish

Compare: Greater Yellowlegs (pg. 157) is much larger and has a longer, slightly upturned bill. The breeding Spotted Sandpiper (pg. 133) has black spots on its chest.

Stan's Notes: Often seen in small flocks, combing shorelines and mudflats in search of food. Usually walks with its head down and tail up, ready to snatch up prey. Uses its long, straight bill to pluck insects and tiny fish out of the water. A member of the sandpiper group known as Tattlers, which scream alarm calls when taking off. Quite often moves into the water before taking flight, and gives a variety of flight notes at takeoff. Nest is a simple depression atop a mound of earth. Nests in marshes in the spruce forests of central Alaska and Canada. Migrates earlier than the Greater Yellowlegs in the fall and later in the spring.

Killdeer

Charadrius vociferus

SUMMER

Size: 11" (28 cm)

Male: An upland shorebird with two black bands around the neck, like a necklace. Brown back and white belly. Bright reddish-orange rump, visible in flight.

Female: same as male

Juvenile: similar to adult, with a single neck band

Nest: ground; male scrapes; 2 broods per year

Eggs: 3–5; tan with brown markings

Incubation: 24–28 days; male and female incubate

Fledging: 25 days; male and female lead their young to food

Migration: complete, to southern states, Mexico and Central America

Food: insects; also worms, snails

Compare: The Spotted Sandpiper (pg. 133) is found around water and lacks the two neck bands of the Killdeer

Stan's Notes: Technically classified as a shorebird but lives in dry habitats instead of the shore. Often found in vacant fields, gravel pits, driveways, wetland edges or along railroad tracks. The only shorebird that has two black neck bands. Known to fake a broken wing to draw intruders away from the nest. Once the nest is safe, the parent will take flight. Nests are just a slight depression in a dry area and are often hard to see. Hatchlings look like miniature adults walking on stilts. Soon after hatching, the young follow their parents around and peck for insects. Gives a loud and distinctive "kill-deer" call. Migrates in small flocks.

Brown Thrasher
Toxostoma rufum

SUMMER

Size: 11" (28 cm)

Male: Rust-red with a long tail. Heavy streaking on the breast and belly. Two white wing bars. Long, curved bill and bright yellow eyes.

Female: same as male

Juvenile: same as adult, but eyes are grayish

Nest: cup; female and male build; 2 broods per year

Eggs: 4–5; pale blue with brown markings

Incubation: 11–14 days; female and male incubate

Fledging: 10–13 days; female and male feed the young

Migration: complete, to southern states

Food: insects, fruit

Compare: Fox Sparrow (pg. 121) has a similar rust-red coloration, but the Thrasher is much larger, thinner, and has a longer bill and tail. Look for the long rust-red tail to help identify the Brown Thrasher.

Stan's Notes: A prodigious songster. Sings along forest edges and in suburban yards. Found in thick shrubs, where it sings deliberate musical phrases, repeating each twice. The male Brown Thrasher has the largest documented repertoire of all North American songbirds, with more than 1,100 types of songs. Builds nest low in dense shrubs, often in fencerows. Quickly flies or runs on the ground in and out of thick shrubs. A noisy feeder due to its habit of turning over leaves, small rocks and branches to find food. More abundant in the central Great Plains than anywhere else in North America.

male

female

Northern Flicker
Colaptes auratus

YEAR-ROUND
SUMMER

Size: 12" (30 cm)

Male: Brown-and-black with a black mustache and black necklace. Red spot on the nape of neck. Speckled chest. Large white rump patch, seen only when flying.

Female: same as male, but lacks a black mustache

Juvenile: same as adult of the same sex

Nest: cavity; female and male excavate; 1 brood per year

Eggs: 5–8; white without markings

Incubation: 11–14 days; female and male incubate

Fledging: 25–28 days; female and male feed the young

Migration: non-migrator in the southern half of the L.P.; partial migrator, to southern states

Food: insects (especially ants and beetles); comes to suet feeders

Compare: The male Yellow-bellied Sapsucker (pg. 49) has a red chin. Male Red-bellied Woodpecker (pg. 55) has a red crown. Flickers are the only brown-backed woodpeckers in Michigan.

Stan's Notes: This is the only woodpecker to regularly feed on the ground. Prefers ants and beetles and produces an antacid saliva that neutralizes the acidic defense of ants. The male often picks the nest site. Parents take up to 12 days to excavate the cavity. Can be attracted to your yard with a nest box stuffed with sawdust. Often reuses an old nest. Undulates deeply during flight, flashing yellow under its wings and tail, and calling "wacka-wacka" loudly.

YEAR-ROUND

Mourning Dove
Zenaida macroura

Size: 12" (30 cm)

Male: Smooth, fawn-colored dove. Gray patch on the head. Iridescent pink and greenish-blue on neck. Single black spot behind and below eyes. Black spots on wings and tail. Pointed, wedged tail with white edges, seen in flight.

Female: similar to male, but lacks the pink-and-green iridescent neck feathers

Juvenile: spotted and streaked plumage

Nest: platform; female and male build; 2 broods per year

Eggs: 2; white without markings

Incubation: 13–14 days; male incubates during the day, female incubates at night

Fledging: 12–14 days; female and male feed the young

Migration: partial to non-migrator; moves around to find food or migrates to southern states

Food: seeds; will visit ground and seed feeders

Compare: Lacks the wide range of color combinations of the Rock Pigeon (pg. 229). Lacks the black collar of the Eurasian Collared-Dove (pg. 227).

Stan's Notes: Name comes from its mournful cooing. A ground feeder, bobbing its head as it walks. One of the few birds to drink without lifting its head, same as the Rock Pigeon. Parents feed the young (squab) a regurgitated liquid called crop milk during their first few days of life. Platform nest is so flimsy, it often falls apart in a storm. During takeoff and in flight, wind rushes through its wing feathers, creating a characteristic whistling sound.

winter

breeding

SUMMER

Pied-billed Grebe
Podilymbus podiceps

Size: 12–14" (30–36 cm)

Male: A small brown waterbird with a black chin and fluffy white patch beneath the tail. Black ring around a thick, chicken-like ivory bill. Winter plumage bill is brown and unmarked.

Female: same as male

Juvenile: paler than the adult, with white spots and a gray chest, belly and bill

Nest: floating platform; female and male build; 1 brood per year

Eggs: 5–7; bluish-white without markings

Incubation: 22–24 days; female and male incubate

Fledging: 45–60 days; female and male feed the young

Migration: complete, to southern states, Mexico and Central America

Food: crayfish, aquatic insects, fish

Compare: Look for the white patch under the tail and the thick bill to help identify the Pied-billed.

Stan's Notes: A summer waterbird in the state, often seen diving for food. When disturbed, slowly sinks like a submarine, quickly compressing its feathers, forcing the air out. Was called Hell-diver due to the length of time it can stay submerged. Able to surface far from where it went under. Well suited to life on water, with short wings, lobed toes, and legs set close to the rear of its body. Swims easily but moves awkwardly on land. Very sensitive to pollution. Builds nest on a floating mat in water. "Grebe" may originate from the Breton word *krib*, meaning "crest," referring to the crested head plumes of many grebes, especially during breeding season.

male
pg. 57

female

MIGRATION

Bufflehead
Bucephala albeola

Size: 13–15" (33–38 cm)

Female: Brownish-gray duck with a dark brown head. White patch on cheek, just behind the eyes.

Male: striking black-and-white duck with a large bonnet-like white patch on the back of head; head shines greenish-purple in sunlight

Juvenile: similar to female

Nest: cavity; female lines an old woodpecker hole; 1 brood per year

Eggs: 8–10; ivory-to-olive without markings

Incubation: 29–31 days; female incubates

Fledging: 50–55 days; female leads the young to food

Migration: complete, to southern states, Mexico and Central America

Food: aquatic insects, crustaceans, mollusks

Compare: The female Common Goldeneye (pg. 173) is very similar, but it is much larger and has a white collar. Look for the white cheek patch to help identify the female Bufflehead.

Stan's Notes: A small, common diving duck, almost always seen in small groups or with other duck species on rivers, ponds and lakes. Nests in vacant woodpecker holes. When cavities in trees are scarce, known to use a burrow in an earthen bank or will use a nest box. Lines the cavity with fluffy down feathers. Unlike other ducks, the young stay in the nest for up to two days before they venture out with their mothers. The female is very territorial and remains with the same mate for many years.

Greater Yellowlegs
Tringa melanoleuca

Size: 13–15" (33–38 cm)

Male: Tall bird with a bulbous head and a long, thin bill, slightly upturned. Gray streaking on the chest. White belly. Long yellow legs.

Female: same as male

Juvenile: same as adult

Nest: ground; female builds; 1 brood per year

Eggs: 3–4; off-white with brown markings

Incubation: 22–23 days; female and male incubate

Fledging: 18–20 days; male and female feed the young

Migration: complete, to southern states, Mexico, Central and South America

Food: small fish, aquatic insects

Compare: Lesser Yellowlegs (pg. 143) is much smaller and has a shorter bill. Killdeer (pg. 145) has two black bands around its neck. Breeding Spotted Sandpiper (pg. 133) has spots on its chest. Look for the long yellow legs and long bill to help identify the Greater Yellowlegs.

Stan's Notes: A common shorebird, often seen during migration. Can be identified by its long legs, which enable it to wade in deep water, and its slightly upturned bill. Often seen resting on one leg. Rushes forward through the water to feed, plowing its bill or swinging it from side to side, catching small fish and insects. A skittish bird, quick to give an alarm call, causing flocks to take flight. Typically moves into the water before taking flight. Gives a variety of "flight" notes at takeoff. Nests on the ground close to water on the northern tundra of Labrador and Newfoundland.

male

female

Green-winged Teal
Anas crecca

SUMMER MIGRATION

Size: 14–15" (36–38 cm)

Male: Chestnut head with a dark green patch outlined with white from the eyes to the nape of neck. Gray body and butter-yellow tail. Green patch on the wings (speculum), seen in flight.

Female: light brown duck with black spots and a green speculum, small bill

Juvenile: same as female

Nest: ground; female builds; 1 brood per year

Eggs: 8–10; cream-white without markings

Incubation: 21–23 days; female incubates

Fledging: 32–34 days; female teaches young to feed

Migration: complete, to southern states and Mexico

Food: aquatic plants and insects

Compare: Female Blue-winged Teal (pg. 161) is similar in size, but it has slight white at the base of its bill. Look for the chestnut head with a dark green patch on each side to identify the male Green-winged Teal.

Stan's Notes: One of the smallest dabbling ducks. Tips forward in water to feed off the bottom of shallow ponds. This behavior makes it vulnerable to ingesting spent lead shot, which can cause death. It walks well on land and will also feed in flooded fields and woodlands. Known for its fast and agile flight. Groups wheel and spin through the air in tight formation. The green wing patches are most obvious during flight.

male

female

Blue-winged Teal
Spatula discors

SUMMER

Size: 15–16" (38–41 cm)

Male: Small, plain-looking brown duck with black speckles and a large, crescent-shaped white mark at the base of bill. Gray head. Black tail with a small white patch. Blue wing patch (speculum), best seen in flight.

Female: duller than the male, with only slight white at the base of bill; lacks a crescent mark on the face and a white patch on the tail

Juvenile: same as female

Nest: ground; female builds; 1 brood per year

Eggs: 8–11; cream-white

Incubation: 23–27 days; female incubates

Fledging: 35–44 days; female feeds the young

Migration: complete, to southern states, Mexico and Central America

Food: aquatic plants, seeds, aquatic insects

Compare: Female Green-winged Teal (pg. 159) lacks white near its bill. Female Mallard (pg. 175) has an orange-and-black bill. Female Wood Duck (pg. 171) has a crest. Look for the white facial mark to identify the male Blue-winged.

Stan's Notes: One of the smallest ducks in North America. Migrates farther than most other ducks. Nesting is widespread, as far north as Alaska. Constructs nest some distance from the water. Female performs a distraction display to protect the nest and young. Male leaves the female near the end of incubation. Planting crops and cultivating to pond edges have caused declining populations.

soaring

SUMMER
MIGRATION

Broad-winged Hawk
Buteo platypterus

Size: 14–19" (36–48 cm); up to 3-ft. wingspan

Male: Brown back and rust-red bars on the breast. Two or three wide black-and-white tail bands. Short, round wings. White under the wings and black "fingertips," seen in flight.

Female: same as male, only slightly larger

Juvenile: tail bands narrower and more numerous, a brown-streaked chest and belly

Nest: platform; female and male build, but female finishes; 1 brood per year

Eggs: 2–3; off-white with brown markings

Incubation: 28–32 days; female incubates, male feeds the female during incubation

Fledging: 34–40 days; female and male feed the young

Migration: complete, to Central and South America

Food: small birds, small mammals, snakes, frogs, toads, large insects

Compare: The Cooper's Hawk (pg. 231) has a longer, thinner tail. Sharp-shinned Hawk (pg. 225) is much smaller. Look for the black-and-white tail bands to identify the Broad-winged.

Stan's Notes: A very common woodland hawk in Michigan. Seen in large groups (kettles) migrating early in fall. Spends most of its time hunting small birds, snakes and frogs in dense woodlands. Short wings help it navigate around forest trees. Often heard before seen. Screams a high-pitched whistle call repetitively when intruders are near the nest. Performs a sky-dance courtship with steep dives, sharp flights upward and rolling over. Very vocal during courtship.

drumming

Ruffed Grouse
Bonasa umbellus

YEAR-ROUND

Size: 16–19" (41–48 cm); up to 2-ft. wingspan

Male: Brown chicken-like bird with a long, squared tail. Wide black band near tip of tail. Tuft of feathers on head (crest) appears like a crown when raised. Black ruffs on the sides of neck.

Female: same as male, but has less obvious neck ruffs

Juvenile: same as female

Nest: ground; female builds; 1 brood per year

Eggs: 9–12; tan with light brown markings

Incubation: 23–24 days; female incubates

Fledging: 10–12 days; female leads the young to food

Migration: non-migrator; moves around to find food

Food: seeds, insects, fruit, leaf buds

Compare: Female Ring-necked Pheasant (pg. 187) is larger and has a longer, pointed tail. Look for the feather tuft on the head and black neck ruffs to help identify the Ruffed Grouse.

Stan's Notes: A common bird of deep woods. Often seen in aspen or other trees, feeding on leaf buds. In the colder northern climates, scaly bristles grow on its feet during winter and serve as snowshoes. When there is enough snow, it dives into a snowbank to roost at night. In spring, the male attracts females by raising its feather tuft, fanning its tail like a turkey and standing on a log, drumming with its wings. The drumming sound is not made by its wings pounding against its chest or hitting the log, but by the air being moved by its cupped wings. Female performs a distraction display to protect her young. There are two color morphs, red and gray. Morph colors show best in the tail. Named for its neck ruffs.

male
pg. 59

female

SUMMER
MIGRATION

Ring-necked Duck
Aythya collaris

Size: 16–19" (41–48 cm)

Female: Brown duck with a darker brown back and crown and lighter brown sides. Gray face. White eye-ring with a white line behind the eye. White ring around the bill. Peaked head.

Male: black head, chest and back, gray-to-white sides, blue bill with a bold white ring and thinner ring at the base, peaked head

Juvenile: similar to female

Nest: ground; female builds; 1 brood per year

Eggs: 8–10; olive-to-brown without markings

Incubation: 26–27 days; female incubates

Fledging: 49–56 days; female teaches the young to feed

Migration: complete, to southern states

Food: aquatic plants and insects

Compare: Female Bufflehead (pg. 155) has a white patch behind its eyes and lacks a ring on its bill. Look for the white ring around the bill to help identify the female Ring-necked Duck.

Stan's Notes: Often seen in pairs in larger freshwater lakes. Usually in small flocks. A diving duck, watch for it to dive underwater to forage for food. Springs up off the water to take flight. It has a distinctive tall, peaked head with a sloped forehead. Flattens its crown when diving. Male gives a quick series of grating barks and grunts. Female gives high-pitched peeps. Named "Ring-necked" for its cinnamon collar, which is nearly impossible to see in the field. Also called Ring-billed Duck due to the white ring on its bill.

male
pg. 61

female

Hooded Merganser
Lophodytes cucullatus

SUMMER

Size: 16–19" (41–48 cm)

Female: Sleek brown-and-rust bird with a red head. Ragged "hair" on the back of head. Long, thin brown bill.

Male: black back, rust-brown sides, long black bill; raises crest "hood" to display a white patch

Juvenile: similar to female

Nest: cavity; female lines an old woodpecker cavity or a nest box near water; 1 brood per year

Eggs: 10–12; white without markings

Incubation: 32–33 days; female incubates

Fledging: 71 days; female feeds the young

Migration: complete, to southern states

Food: small fish, aquatic insects and crustaceans (especially crayfish)

Compare: The female Common Merganser (pg. 271) is much larger and has a white chin and orange bill. Look for the ragged "hair" on the back of the head to help identify the female Hoodie.

Stan's Notes: A small diving duck, found in shallow ponds, sloughs, lakes and rivers. Usually in small groups. Quick, low flight across the water, with fast wingbeats. Male has a deep, rolling call. Female gives a hoarse quack. Nests in wooded areas. Female will lay some eggs in the nests of other mergansers, goldeneyes or Wood Ducks (egg dumping), resulting in 20–25 eggs in some nests. Rarely, she shares a nest, sitting with a Wood Duck.

male
pg. 245

female

SUMMER

Wood Duck
Aix sponsa

Size: 17–20" (43–51 cm)

Female: A small brown dabbling duck. Bright white eye-ring and a not-so-obvious crest. Blue patch on wings (speculum), often hidden.

Male: highly ornamented with a mostly green head and crest patterned with black-and-white, a rusty chest, white belly and red eyes

Juvenile: similar to female

Nest: cavity; female lines an old woodpecker cavity or a nest box in a tree; 1 brood per year

Eggs: 10–15; cream-white without markings

Incubation: 28–36 days; female incubates

Fledging: 56–68 days; female teaches the young to feed

Migration: complete, to southern states

Food: aquatic insects, plants, seeds

Compare: Female Mallard (pg. 175) and female Blue-winged Teal (pg. 161) lack the bright white eye-ring and crest. Female Northern Shoveler (pg. 177) has a large spoon-shaped bill.

Stan's Notes: A common duck of quiet, shallow backwater ponds. Nearly went extinct around 1900 due to overhunting, but it's doing well now. Nests in a tree cavity or a nest box in a tree. Seen flying in forests or perching on high branches. Female takes off with a loud squealing call and enters the nest cavity from full flight. Lays some eggs in a neighboring nest (egg dumping), resulting in excess of 20 eggs in some clutches. Hatchlings stay in the nest for 24 hours, then jump from as high up as 60 feet (18 m) to the ground or water to follow their mother. They never return to the nest.

male
pg. 63

female

Common Goldeneye

Bucephala clangula

SUMMER
MIGRATION
WINTER

Size: 18–20" (45–51 cm)

Female: A brown-and-gray duck with a large dark brown head and gray body. White collar. Bright golden eyes. Yellow-tipped dark bill.

Male: mostly white with a black back, puffy green head, large white spot on the face, bright golden eyes and dark bill

Juvenile: same as female, but has a dark bill

Nest: cavity; female lines an old woodpecker hole; 1 brood per year

Eggs: 8–10; light green without markings

Incubation: 28–32 days; female incubates

Fledging: 56–59 days; female leads the young to food

Migration: complete, to southern states and Mexico

Food: aquatic plants, insects, fish, mollusks

Compare: Female Bufflehead (pg. 155) is much smaller and has a white patch on its cheeks. Look for the dark brown head and white collar to help identify the female Common Goldeneye.

Stan's Notes: Known for the loud whistling sound produced by its wings during flight. During late winter and early spring, the male performs elaborate mating displays that include throwing his head back and calling a raspy note. Female will lay some of her eggs in other goldeneye nests or in the nests of other species (egg dumping), causing some mothers to incubate as many as 30 eggs in a brood. Named for its obvious bright golden eyes.

male
pg. 249

female

Mallard
Anas platyrhynchos

SUMMER

Size:	19–21" (48–53 cm)
Female:	Brown duck with an orange-and-black bill and blue-and-white wing mark (speculum).
Male:	large green head, white necklace, rust-brown or chestnut chest, combination of gray-and-white sides, yellow bill, orange legs and feet
Juvenile:	same as female, but with a yellow bill
Nest:	ground; female builds; 1 brood per year
Eggs:	7–10; greenish-to-whitish, unmarked
Incubation:	26–30 days; female incubates
Fledging:	42–52 days; female leads the young to food
Migration:	complete, to southern states; some stay in Michigan and do not migrate
Food:	seeds, plants, aquatic insects; will come to ground feeders offering corn
Compare:	The female Northern Shoveler (pg. 177) is smaller and has a large spoon-shaped bill. The female Wood Duck (pg. 171) has a white eye-ring. Female Blue-winged Teal (pg. 161) is smaller than the female Mallard.

Stan's Notes: A familiar dabbling duck of lakes and ponds. Also found in rivers, streams and some backyards. Tips forward to feed on vegetation on the bottom of shallow water. The name "Mallard" comes from the Latin word *masculus,* meaning "male," referring to the male's habit of taking no part in raising the young. Female and male have white underwings and white tails, but only the male has black central tail feathers that curl upward. The female gives a classic quack. Returns to its birthplace each year.

male
pg. 251

female

Northern Shoveler

Spatula clypeata

MIGRATION

Size: 19–21" (48–53 cm)

Female: A medium-sized brown duck speckled with black. Green patch on the wings (speculum). An extraordinarily large, spoon-shaped bill.

Male: iridescent green head, rusty sides, white chest and a large spoon-shaped bill

Juvenile: same as female

Nest: ground; female builds; 1 brood per year

Eggs: 9–12; olive without markings

Incubation: 22–25 days; female incubates

Fledging: 30–60 days; female leads the young to food

Migration: complete, to southern states, Mexico and Central America

Food: aquatic insects, plants

Compare: The female Wood Duck (pg. 171) is smaller and has a white eye-ring. The female Mallard (pg. 175) lacks the large bill. Look for the spoon-shaped bill to identify the Shoveler.

Stan's Notes: One of several species of shovelers. Called "Shoveler" due to the peculiar, shovel-like shape of its bill. Given the common name "Northern" because it is the only species of these ducks in North America. Seen in shallow wetlands, ponds and small lakes in flocks of 5–10 birds. Flocks fly in tight formation. Swims low in water, pointing its large bill toward the water as if it's too heavy to lift. Usually swims in tight circles while feeding. Feeds mainly by filtering tiny aquatic insects and plants from the surface of the water with its bill. Female gathers plant material and forms it into a nest a short distance from the water.

male
pg. 235

female

soaring

Northern Harrier
Circus hudsonius

YEAR-ROUND
SUMMER

Size: 18–22" (45–56 cm); up to 4-ft. wingspan

Female: A slender, low-flying hawk with a dark brown back and brown streaking on the chest and belly. Large white rump patch. Thin black tail bands and black wing tips. Yellow eyes.

Male: silver-gray with a large white rump patch and white belly, faint thin bands across tail, black wing tips and yellow eyes

Juvenile: similar to female, with an orange chest

Nest: ground; female and male construct; 1 brood per year

Eggs: 4–8; bluish-white without markings

Incubation: 31–32 days; female incubates

Fledging: 30–35 days; male and female feed the young

Migration: complete, to southern states, Mexico and Central America; some don't migrate

Food: mice, snakes, insects, small birds

Compare: Slimmer than the Red-tailed Hawk (pg. 181). Look for the characteristic low gliding and the black tail bands to identify the female Harrier.

Stan's Notes: One of the easiest of hawks to identify. Glides just aboveground, following the contours of the land while searching for prey. Holds its wings just above the horizontal position, tilting back and forth in the wind, similar to Turkey Vultures. Formerly called Marsh Hawk due to its habit of hunting over marshes. Feeds and nests on the ground. Will also preen and rest on the ground. Unlike other hawks, mainly uses its hearing to find prey, followed by eyesight. At any age, it has a distinctive owl-like face disk.

soaring

YEAR-ROUND
SUMMER

Red-tailed Hawk
Buteo jamaicensis

Size: 19–23" (48–58 cm); up to 4½-ft. wingspan

Male: A variety of colorations from chocolate-brown to nearly all white. Often brown with a white breast and brown belly band. Rust-red tail. Underside of wing is white with a small dark patch on the leading edge near the shoulder.

Female: same as male, only slightly larger

Juvenile: similar to adults, with a speckled breast and light eyes; lacks a red tail

Nest: platform; male and female build; 1 brood per year

Eggs: 2–3; white without markings or sometimes marked with brown

Incubation: 30–35 days; female and male incubate

Fledging: 45–46 days; male and female feed the young

Migration: partial to non-migrator; will move around in winter to find food

Food: small and medium-sized animals, large birds, snakes, fish, insects, bats, carrion

Compare: Female Northern Harrier (pg. 179) is slimmer and lacks the red tail.

Stan's Notes: Common in open country and cities. Seen perching on fences, freeway light posts and trees. Look for it circling above open fields and roadsides, searching for prey. Gives a high-pitched scream that trails off. Often builds a large stick nest in large trees along roads. Lines nest with finer material, like evergreen needles. Returns to the same nest site each year. The red tail develops in the second year and is best seen from above.

YEAR-ROUND

Barred Owl
Strix varia

Size: 20–24" (51–61 cm); up to 3½-ft. wingspan

Male: A chunky brown-and-gray owl with a large head and dark brown eyes. Dark horizontal barring on upper chest. Vertical streaks on lower chest and belly. Yellow bill and feet.

Female: same as male, only slightly larger

Juvenile: light gray with a black face

Nest: cavity; doesn't add nesting material; 1 brood per year

Eggs: 2–3; white without markings

Incubation: 28–33 days; female incubates

Fledging: 42–44 days; female and male feed the young

Migration: non-migrator

Food: mice, rabbits and other animals, small birds, fish, reptiles, amphibians

Compare: Lacks the "horns" of the Great Horned Owl (pg. 185) and the "ears" of the much smaller Eastern Screech Owl (pg. 213). Look for a stocky owl with a large head and dark brown eyes to identify the Barred Owl.

Stan's Notes: A very common owl in the state. Prefers deciduous, dense woodlands with sparse undergrowth, but it can be attracted to your yard with a simple nest box that has a large entrance hole. Often seen hunting during the day. Perches and watches for mice, birds and other prey. Hovers over water and reaches down to grab a fish. After fledging, the young stay with their parents for up to four months. Often sounds like a dog barking just before calling 6–8 hoots, sounding like "who-who-who-cooks-for-you."

YEAR-ROUND

Great Horned Owl
Bubo virginianus

Size: 21–25" (53–64 cm); up to 4-ft. wingspan

Male: A robust brown "horned" owl. Bright yellow eyes and V-shaped white throat, resembling a necklace. Horizontal barring on the chest.

Female: same as male, only slightly larger

Juvenile: similar to adults, but lacks ear tufts

Nest: no nest; takes over the nest of a crow, hawk or Great Blue Heron, or uses a partial cavity, stump or broken tree; 1 brood per year

Eggs: 2–3; white without markings

Incubation: 26–30 days; female incubates

Fledging: 30–35 days; male and female feed the young

Migration: non-migrator

Food: mammals, birds (ducks), snakes, insects

Compare: Barred Owl (pg. 183) is stocky and has dark eyes. Eastern Screech-Owl (pg. 213) is extremely tiny. Look for the bright yellow eyes and feather "horns" on the head to help identify the Great Horned Owl.

Stan's Notes: One of the earliest nesting birds in Michigan, laying eggs in January and February. Can hear a mouse move beneath a leaf pile or a foot of snow. "Ears" are tufts of feathers (horns) and have nothing to do with hearing. Cannot turn its head all the way around. Wing feathers are ragged on the ends, resulting in silent flight. Eyelids close from the top down, like ours. Fearless, it is one of the few animals that will kill skunks and porcupines. Given that, it is also called Flying Tiger. Call sounds like "hoo-hoo-hoo-hoooo."

YEAR-ROUND

Ring-necked Pheasant
Phasianus colchicus

Size: 30–36" (76–91 cm), male, including tail
21–25" (53–64 cm), female, including tail

Male: Golden-brown body with a long tail. White ring around the neck. Head is purple, green, blue and red.

Female: smaller and less flamboyant than the male, with brown plumage and a long tail

Juvenile: similar to female, with a shorter tail

Nest: ground; female builds; 1 brood per year

Eggs: 8–10; olive-brown without markings

Incubation: 23–25 days; female incubates

Fledging: 11–12 days; female leads the young to food

Migration: non-migrator; moves around to find food

Food: insects, seeds, fruit; visits ground feeders

Compare: Both male and female Ring-necked Pheasants have long tails, but the male is much larger and brightly colored.

Stan's Notes: Originally introduced to North America from China in the late 1800s. Common now throughout the U.S. Like many other game birds, its numbers vary greatly, making it common in some years, scarce in others. Seeks shelter during harsh winter weather. To attract females, the male gives a cackling call, and then rapidly flutters his wings. Usually walks or runs. Takes off in an explosive flight with fast wingbeats followed by gliding low to the ground. Roosts on the ground or in trees at night. The name "Ring-necked" refers to the white ring around the male's neck. "Pheasant" comes from the Greek word *phaisianos*, which means "bird of the River Phasis" (known today as the Rioni River).

displaying male

non-displaying

female

Wild Turkey
Meleagris gallopavo

YEAR-ROUND

Size: 36–48" (91–122 cm)

Male: A large brown-and-bronze bird with a naked blue-and-red head. Long, straight black beard in the center of chest. Tail spreads open like a fan. Spurs on legs.

Female: thinner and less striking than the male; often lacks a breast beard

Juvenile: same as adult of the same sex

Nest: ground; female builds; 1 brood per year

Eggs: 10–12; buff-white with dull brown markings

Incubation: 27–28 days; female incubates

Fledging: 6–10 days; female leads the young to food

Migration: non-migrator; moves around to find food

Food: insects, seeds, fruit

Compare: This bird is quite distinctive and unlikely to be confused with any other.

Stan's Notes: This is the largest native game bird in Michigan, and the species from which the domestic turkey was bred. A strong flier that can approach 60 mph (97 kph). Can fly straight up, then away. Eyesight is three times better than ours. Hearing is also excellent; can hear competing males up to a mile away. Male has a "harem" of up to 20 females. Female scrapes out a depression for nesting and pads it with soft leaves. Males are known as toms, females are hens, young are poults. Roosts in trees at night. It was eliminated from Michigan due to market hunting and loss of habitat, and reintroduced during the 1950–60s. Populations are now stable.

Ruby-crowned Kinglet

Regulus calendula

SUMMER MIGRATION

Size: 4" (10 cm)

Male: A small, teardrop-shaped green-to-gray bird. Two white wing bars and a white eye-ring. Hidden ruby crown.

Female: same as male, but lacks a ruby crown

Juvenile: same as female

Nest: pendulous; female builds; 1 brood per year

Eggs: 4–5; white with brown markings

Incubation: 11–12 days; female incubates

Fledging: 11–12 days; female and male feed the young

Migration: complete, to southern states, Mexico and Central America

Food: insects, berries

Compare: Golden-crowned Kinglet (pg. 193) lacks a ruby crown. The female American Goldfinch (pg. 287) is similar, but it is larger. Look for the white eye-ring of the Ruby-crowned.

Stan's Notes: One of the smallest birds in Michigan. Most commonly seen during migration, when groups travel together. Watch for it flitting in thick shrubs low to the ground. It takes a quick eye to see the ruby crown, which the male flashes when he is excited. The female weaves an unusually intricate nest and fastens colorful lichens and mosses to the exterior with spiderwebs. Often builds the nest high in a mature tree, where it hangs from a branch that has overlapping leaves. Sings a distinctive song that starts out soft and ends loud and on a higher note. "Kinglet" originates from the Anglo-Saxon word *cyning*, or "king," referring to the male's red crown, and the diminutive suffix "let," meaning "small."

male

female

SUMMER MIGRATION

Golden-crowned Kinglet
Regulus satrapa

Size: 4" (10 cm)

Male: Tiny, plump green-to-gray bird. Distinctive yellow-and-orange patch with a black border on the crown (see inset). A white eyebrow mark. Two white wing bars.

Female: same as male, but has a yellow crown with a black border, lacks any orange (see inset)

Juvenile: same as adults, but lacks gold on the crown

Nest: pendulous; female constructs; 1–2 broods per year

Eggs: 5–9; white or creamy with brown markings

Incubation: 14–15 days; female incubates

Fledging: 14–19 days; female and male feed young

Migration: complete, to southern states, Mexico and Central America

Food: insects, fruit, tree sap

Compare: Similar to Ruby-crowned Kinglet (pg. 191), but Golden-crowned has an obvious crown. Smaller than the female American Goldfinch (pg. 287), which has an all-black forehead.

Stan's Notes: A breeding resident in the U.P. and in northern parts of the L.P. Common during migration. Often seen in flocks with chickadees, nuthatches, woodpeckers, Brown Creepers and Ruby-crowned Kinglets. Flicks its wings when moving around. Constructs an unusual hanging nest, often with moss, lichens and spiderwebs, and lines it with bark and feathers. Can have so many eggs in its small nest that eggs are in two layers. Drinks tree sap and feeds by gleaning insects from trees. Can be very tame and approachable.

male

female

Red-breasted Nuthatch
Sitta canadensis

YEAR-ROUND
WINTER

Size: 4½" (11 cm)

Male: Gray-backed bird with an obvious black eye line and black cap. Rust-red breast and belly.

Female: duller than the male and has a gray cap and pale undersides

Juvenile: same as female

Nest: cavity; male and female excavate a cavity or move into a vacant hole; 1 brood per year

Eggs: 5–6; white with red-brown markings

Incubation: 11–12 days; female incubates

Fledging: 14–20 days; female and male feed the young

Migration: irruptive; moves around in search of food

Food: insects, insect eggs, seeds; comes to seed and suet feeders

Compare: White-breasted Nuthatch (pg. 199) is larger and has a white breast. Look for the rust-red breast and black eye line to help identify the Red-breasted Nuthatch.

Stan's Notes: The nuthatch climbs down trunks of trees headfirst, searching for insects. Like a chickadee, it grabs a seed from a feeder and flies off to crack it open. Wedges the seed into a crevice and pounds it open with several sharp blows. The name "Nuthatch" comes from the Middle English moniker *nuthak*, referring to the habit of hacking seeds open. Look for it in mature conifers, where it extracts seeds from pinecones. Excavates a cavity or takes an old woodpecker hole or a natural cavity and builds a nest within. An irruptive migrator, common in some winters and scarce in others. Gives a series of nasal "yank-yank-yank" calls.

Boreal
Chickadee

YEAR-ROUND

Black-capped Chickadee
Poecile atricapillus

Size: 5" (13 cm)

Male: Familiar gray bird with a black cap and throat patch. Tan sides and belly. White chest. Small white wing marks.

Female: same as male

Juvenile: same as adult

Nest: cavity; female and male excavate or use a nest box; 1 brood per year

Eggs: 5–7; white with fine brown markings

Incubation: 11–13 days; female and male incubate

Fledging: 14–18 days; female and male feed the young

Migration: non-migrator; moves around to find food

Food: seeds, insects, fruit; will come to seed and suet feeders

Compare: Boreal Chickadee (see inset) is very similar, but it has a brown cap. The Tufted Titmouse (pg. 205) is larger and has a crest.

Stan's Notes: A perky backyard bird that can be attracted with a nest box or bird feeder. Usually the first to find a new seed or suet feeder. Can be easily tamed and hand fed. Much of the diet comes from bird feeders, so it can be a common urban bird. Needs to feed every day in winter and forages to find food even during the worst winter storms. Typically seen with nuthatches, woodpeckers and other birds. Builds nest mostly with green moss and lines it with fur. Named "Chickadee" for its familiar "chika-dee-dee-dee-dee" call. Also gives a high-pitched, two-toned "fee-bee" call. Can have different calls in different regions. The similar-looking Boreal Chickadee is uncommon and found in northern Michigan.

197

White-breasted Nuthatch
Sitta carolinensis

YEAR-ROUND

Size: 5–6" (13–15 cm)

Male: Slate-gray with a white face, breast and belly, and a large white patch on the rump. Black cap and nape of neck. Bill is long and thin, slightly upturned. Chestnut undertail.

Female: similar to male, but has a gray cap and nape

Juvenile: similar to female

Nest: cavity; female and male build a nest within; 1 brood per year

Eggs: 5–7; white with brown markings

Incubation: 11–12 days; female incubates

Fledging: 13–14 days; female and male feed the young

Migration: non-migrator

Food: insects, insect eggs, seeds; comes to seed and suet feeders

Compare: Red-breasted Nuthatch (pg. 195) is smaller and has a rust-red belly and distinctive black eye line. Look for the white breast to help identify the White-breasted Nuthatch.

Stan's Notes: The nuthatch hops headfirst down trees, looking for insects that birds climbing up miss. Its climbing agility is due to an extra-long hind toe claw, or nail, that is nearly twice the size of its front claws. "Nuthatch," from the Middle English *nuthak,* refers to the bird's habit of wedging a seed in a crevice and hacking it open. Often seen in flocks with chickadees, Brown Creepers and Downy Woodpeckers. Mates stay together year-round, defending a small territory. Gives a characteristic "whi-whi-whi-whi" spring call during February and March.

male

female

first winter

Yellow-rumped Warbler

Setophaga coronata

Size: 5–6" (13–15 cm)

Male: Slate-gray with black streaking on the chest. Yellow patches on the head, flanks and rump. White chin and belly. Two white wing bars.

Female: duller gray than the male, mixed with brown

Juvenile: first winter is similar to the adult female

Nest: cup; female builds; 2 broods per year

Eggs: 4–5; white with brown markings

Incubation: 12–13 days; female incubates

Fledging: 10–12 days; female and male feed the young

Migration: complete, to southern states, Mexico and Central America

Food: insects, berries; visits suet feeders in spring

Compare: The male Yellow Warbler (pg. 293) is yellow with orange streaking on its chest. Chestnut-sided Warbler (pg. 87) has chestnut flanks and lacks the yellow rump. Look for yellow patches to help identify the Yellow rumped.

Stan's Notes: One of the first warblers to return in spring and one of the last to leave in fall. Seems to prefer deciduous woods and forest edges but seen in any habitat during migration. Familiar call is a single robust "chip," heard mostly during migration. Sings a wonderful song in spring. Comes to suet feeders in spring, when insect populations are low. Moves quickly among trees and from the ground to trees. Flits around the upper branches of tall trees. In the fall, the male molts to a dull color similar to the female, but he retains his yellow patches all year. Also called Myrtle Warbler. Sometimes called Butterbutt due to the yellow patch on its rump.

female
pg. 107

male

YEAR-ROUND
WINTER

Dark-eyed Junco
Junco hyemalis

Size: 5½" (14 cm)

Male: A plump, dark-eyed bird with a slate-gray-to-charcoal chest, head and back. White belly. Pink bill. White outer tail feathers appear like a white V in flight.

Female: round bird with brown plumage

Juvenile: similar to female, with streaking on the breast and head

Nest: cup; female and male build; 2 broods per year

Eggs: 3–5; white with reddish-brown markings

Incubation: 12–13 days; female incubates

Fledging: 10–13 days; male and female feed the young

Migration: complete, to most of Michigan and across the U.S.

Food: seeds, insects; visits ground and seed feeders

Compare: Rarely confused with any other bird. Look for the pink bill and small flocks feeding beneath seed feeders to identify the male Dark-eyed Junco.

Stan's Notes: One of the most common winter birds in the state. Migrates from Canada and northern parts of Michigan to areas farther south. Adheres to a rigid social hierarchy, with dominant birds chasing the less-dominant birds. Look for the white outer tail feathers flashing in flight. Often seen in small flocks on the ground, where it uses its feet to simultaneously "double-scratch" to expose seeds and insects. Eats many weed seeds. Nests in a wide variety of wooded habitats. Several subspecies of Dark-eyed Junco were previously considered to be separate species.

YEAR-ROUND

Tufted Titmouse
Baeolophus bicolor

Size: 6" (15 cm)

Male: Slate-gray bird with a white chest and belly. Pointed crest. Rust-brown wash on flanks. Gray legs and dark eyes.

Female: same as male

Juvenile: same as adult

Nest: cavity; female lines an old woodpecker cavity; 2 broods per year

Eggs: 5–7; white with brown markings

Incubation: 13–14 days; female incubates

Fledging: 15–18 days; female and male feed the young

Migration: non-migrator

Food: insects, seeds, fruit; will come to seed and suet feeders

Compare: Black-capped Chickadee (pg. 197) is a close relative, but it is smaller and lacks a crest. The White-breasted Nuthatch (pg. 199) has a rust-brown undertail. Look for the pointed crest to help identify the Tufted Titmouse.

Stan's Notes: A common feeder bird that can be attracted with an offering of black oil sunflower seeds or suet. Can also be attracted with a nest box. Well known for its "peter-peter-peter" call, which it quickly repeats. Notorious for pulling hair from sleeping dogs, cats and squirrels to line its nest. Usually seen only one or two at a time. Male feeds the female during courtship and nesting. The prefix "Tit" in the common name comes from a Scandinavian word meaning "little." Suffix "mouse" is derived from the Old English word *mase*, meaning "bird." Simply translated, it is a "small bird."

Eastern Phoebe
Sayornis phoebe

SUMMER

Size: 7" (18 cm)

Male: Plain gray bird with slightly darker wings, a light olive-green belly and thin dark bill.

Female: same as male

Juvenile: same as adult

Nest: cup; female builds; 2 broods per year

Eggs: 4–5; white without markings

Incubation: 15–16 days; female incubates

Fledging: 15–16 days; male and female feed the young

Migration: complete, to southern states and Mexico

Food: insects

Compare: Gray Catbird (pg. 217) has a black crown and a chestnut patch under its tail. The Eastern Phoebe lacks any distinctive markings. Listen for its well-enunciated "fee-bee" call and look for the hawking and tail-pumping behaviors to help identify this bird.

Stan's Notes: A sparrow-sized bird that often perches on the end of a dead branch. Found in forests, yards and farms. In a process called hawking, it waits for a passing insect. When a bug flies near, it launches out to catch it, and then returns to the same branch. It has a very distinctive habit of pumping its tail up and down while perching. Builds a nest beneath the eaves of a house, under a bridge or in another sheltered spot. Uses mud, grass and moss for nest materials and hair (and sometimes feathers) for the lining. The common name is derived from its very distinct "fee-bee" call, which it repeats over and over from the top of dead branches.

Eastern Kingbird
Tyrannus tyrannus

SUMMER

Size: 8" (20 cm)

Male: Mostly gray-and-black with a white chin and belly. Black head and tail with a distinct white band on the tip of tail. Concealed red crown, rarely seen.

Female: same as male

Juvenile: same as adult

Nest: cup; male and female build; 1 brood per year

Eggs: 3–4; white with brown markings

Incubation: 16–18 days; female incubates

Fledging: 16–18 days; female and male feed the young

Migration: complete, to Mexico, Central America and South America

Food: insects, fruit

Compare: American Robin (pg. 219) is larger and has a rust-red breast. Eastern Phoebe (pg. 207) is smaller and has an olive-green belly. Look for the white tail band to identify the Kingbird.

Stan's Notes: A summer resident in open fields and prairies. As many as 20 birds migrate with each other in a group. Returns to the mating ground in spring, where pairs defend their territory. Seems to be unafraid of other birds and chases larger birds. Given the common name "King" for its bold attitude and behavior. In a hunting technique known as hawking, it perches on a branch and watches for insects, flies out to catch one, and then returns to the same perch. Swoops from perch to perch when hunting. Becomes very vocal during late summer, when family members call back and forth to each other while hunting for insects.

Great Crested Flycatcher
Myiarchus crinitus

SUMMER

Size: 8" (20 cm)

Male: Gray head with a prominent crest. Gray back and throat. Yellow from the belly to the base of a reddish-brown tail. Lower bill is yellow at the base.

Female: same as male

Juvenile: same as adult

Nest: cavity; female and male stuff a vacant woodpecker cavity or nest box; 1 brood per year

Eggs: 4–6; white-to-buff with brown markings

Incubation: 13–15 days; female incubates

Fledging: 14–21 days; female and male feed the young

Migration: complete, to Mexico and Central America

Food: insects, fruit

Compare: The Eastern Kingbird (pg. 209) has a white band across its tail. Eastern Phoebe (pg. 207) is similar, but it lacks a crest and yellow belly. Look for the crest to identify the Flycatcher.

Stan's Notes: A common bird of wooded areas throughout the state. It lives high up in trees, rarely coming to ground. Makes long flights from treetop to treetop, moving from one hunting area to another. Gleans insects from tree leaves. Often heard before seen. "Great Crested" refers to the set of extra-long feathers on top of its head (crest), which the bird raises when alert or agitated, like the Northern Cardinal. Nests in an old woodpecker hole but can be attracted with a man-made nest box that has an entrance hole 1½–2½ inches (4–6 cm) in diameter. Often stuffs the cavity with a collection of fur, feathers, string and snakeskins.

red morph

gray morph

YEAR-ROUND

Eastern Screech-Owl
Megascops asio

Size: 8–10" (20–25 cm); up to 2-ft. wingspan

Male: A small "eared" owl that occurs in different colorations. Gray morph is mottled gray-and-white. Red morph is mottled rust-and-white. Short wings. Bright yellow eyes.

Female: same as male, only slightly larger

Juvenile: lighter color than adults of the same morph and usually lacks ear tufts

Nest: cavity, old woodpecker cavity or man-made nest box; does not add any nesting material; 1 brood per year

Eggs: 4–5; white without markings

Incubation: 25–26 days; female incubates, male feeds the female during incubation

Fledging: 26–27 days; male and female feed the young

Migration: non-migrator; moves around in winter

Food: large insects, small mammals, birds, snakes

Compare: Hard to confuse with the much larger Great Horned Owl (pg. 185). The Screech-Owl is the only small owl in Michigan with ear tufts.

Stan's Notes: Commonly found in forests that have suitable natural cavities for nesting and roosting. Active from dusk to dawn. Usually gives a tremulous, descending trill, like a sound effect in a scary movie. Seldom gives a screeching call. Often seen sunning itself at a nest box hole during winter. Mates may have a long-term pair bond and may roost together at night. Excellent hearing and eyesight. Flaps rapidly and flies silently. Has winter and summer territories. The gray morph is more common than the red.

male
pg. 269

female

WINTER

Pine Grosbeak
Pinicola enucleator

Size: 9" (23 cm)

Female: Plump gray finch with a long dark tail. Dark wings with two white wing bars. Head and rump have a dull yellow tinge. Short, pointed dark bill.

Male: plump bird, overall rose-red and gray

Juvenile: female is similar to the adult female; male has a touch of red on the head and rump

Nest: cup; female builds; 1 brood per year

Eggs: 4–5; bluish-green without markings

Incubation: 13–15 days; female incubates

Fledging: 13–20 days; female and male feed the young

Migration: irruptive; moves around the U.P. and northern parts of the L.P. in winter to find food

Food: seeds, fruit, insects; will come to seed feeders

Compare: The female Evening Grosbeak (pg. 301) is slightly smaller and lacks the dull yellow head of the female Pine Grosbeak.

Stan's Notes: A very tame and approachable seed eater. Common in some winters and not so common in others. Often seen along roads or on the ground, eating tiny grains of sand and dirt, which help aid digestion. Favors coniferous woods, rarely moving out of coniferous regions during summer, but also likes mixed forests. Will bathe in fluffy snow. Flies in a typical finch-like undulating pattern while giving soft, whistle "cheer" calls. Male sings a rich, beautiful song all year long. Male and female develop a pouch in the bottom of their mouths (buccal pouch) during the breeding season for transporting seeds to their young.

Gray Catbird
Dumetella carolinensis

SUMMER

Size:	9" (23 cm)
Male:	Handsome slate-gray bird with a black crown and a long, thin black bill. Often lifts up its tail, exposing a chestnut patch beneath.
Female:	same as male
Juvenile:	same as adult
Nest:	cup; female and male build; 2 broods per year
Eggs:	4–6; blue-green without markings
Incubation:	12–13 days; female incubates
Fledging:	10–11 days; female and male feed the young
Migration:	complete, to southern states, Mexico and Central America
Food:	insects, occasional fruit; visits suet feeders
Compare:	Eastern Phoebe (pg. 207) is smaller and has an olive belly. Eastern Kingbird (pg. 209) has a similar size, but it has a white belly and white band across its tail. To help identify the Gray Catbird, look for the black crown and a chestnut patch under the tail.

Stan's Notes: A secretive bird, more often heard than seen. The Chippewa Indians gave it a name that means "the bird that cries with grief" due to its raspy call. Called "Catbird" because the sound is like the meowing of a house cat. Often mimics other birds, rarely repeating the same phrases. Found in forest edges, backyards and parks. Builds its nest with small twigs. Nests in thick shrubs and quickly flies back into shrubs if approached. If a cowbird lays an egg in its nest, the catbird will quickly break it and eject it.

male

female

American Robin

Turdus migratorius

SUMMER

Size: 9–11" (23–28 cm)

Male: Familiar gray bird with a dark rust-red breast and a nearly black head and tail. White chin with black streaks. White eye-ring.

Female: similar to male, with a duller rust-red breast and gray head

Juvenile: similar to female, with a speckled breast and brown back

Nest: cup; female builds with help from the male; 2–3 broods per year

Eggs: 4–7; pale blue without markings

Incubation: 12–14 days; female incubates

Fledging: 14–16 days; female and male feed the young

Migration: complete, to southern states, Mexico, Central America; small percentage won't migrate

Food: insects, fruit, berries, earthworms

Compare: Familiar bird to all. To differentiate the male from the female, compare the nearly black head and rust-red chest of the male with the gray head and duller chest of the female.

Stan's Notes: Can be heard singing all night in spring. City robins sing louder than country robins in order to hear each other over traffic and noise. A robin isn't listening for worms when it turns its head to one side. It is focusing its sight out of one eye to look for dirt moving, which is caused by worms moving. Territorial, often fighting its own reflection in a window. Some Michigan robins stay in low, swampy areas during winter, feeding on leftover berries and insect eggs. Some of these non-migrators will die before spring.

displaying

SUMMER
MIGRATION

Northern Mockingbird
Mimus polyglottos

Size: 10" (25 cm)

Male: Silver-gray head and back with a light gray breast and belly. White wing patches, seen in flight or during display. Tail mostly black with white outer tail feathers. Black bill.

Female: same as male

Juvenile: dull gray, a heavily streaked breast, gray bill

Nest: cup; female and male construct; 2 broods per year, sometimes more

Eggs: 3–5; blue green with brown markings

Incubation: 12–13 days; female incubates

Fledging: 11–13 days; female and male feed young

Migration: complete, to southern states

Food: insects, fruit

Compare: The Gray Catbird (pg. 217) is slate gray and lacks wing patches. Look for Mockingbird to spread its wings, flash its white wing patches and wag its tail from side to side.

Stan's Notes: A very animated bird. Performs an elaborate mating dance. Facing each other with heads and tails erect, pairs will run toward each other, flashing their white wing patches, and then retreat to cover nearby. Thought to flash its wing patches as it hunts, which scares and flushes up insects. Sits for long periods on top of a shrub. Imitates other birds (vocal mimicry), hence the common name. Young males often sing at night. Often unafraid of people, allowing for close observation.

Canada Jay
Perisoreus canadensis

YEAR-ROUND

Size: 11½" (29 cm)

Male: Large gray bird with a black nape and white chest. White patch on forehead. Short black bill and dark eyes.

Female: same as male

Juvenile: soot-gray plumage with a faint white whisker mark on each side of the face

Nest: cup; male and female build; 1 brood per year

Eggs: 3–4; grayish-white with fine markings or may be unmarked

Incubation: 16–18 days; female incubates

Fledging: 14–15 days; male and female feed the young

Migration: non-migrator; moves around to find food

Food: insects, seeds, fruit, nuts; visits seed feeders

Compare: Blue Jay (pg. 83) has a similar size, but it has a crest and blue coloring. Look for the white forehead to help identify the Canada Jay.

Stan's Notes: A bird of northern woods. Likes evergreen forests, mixed woods and campsites. Travels around in small family units of 3–5 birds, making good company for campers. Reminds some people of an overgrown chickadee. Also called Camp Robber because it rummages through camps, looking for scraps of food. Also known as Gray Jay or Whiskey Jack. Easily tamed, it will fly to your hand if offered raisins or nuts. Will eat just about anything. Stores extra food for the winter, balling it together in a sticky mass, and then placing it on a tree branch, often concealing it with lichen or bark. Doesn't vocalize much but will give a variety of chatters and whistles.

soaring

juvenile

SUMMER

Sharp-shinned Hawk
Accipiter striatus

Size: 10–14" (25–36 cm); up to 2-ft. wingspan

Male: Small woodland hawk with a gray back and head and rust-red chest. Short wings. A long, squared tail and several dark tail bands, with the widest band at the end of tail. Red eyes.

Female: same as male, only larger

Juvenile: same size as adults, with a brown back, heavy streaking on the chest and yellow eyes

Nest: platform; female builds; 1 brood per year

Eggs: 4–5; white with brown markings

Incubation: 32–35 days; female incubates

Fledging: 24–27 days; female and male feed the young

Migration: complete, to southern states, Mexico and Central America

Food: birds, small mammals

Compare: Cooper's Hawk (pg. 231) is much larger and has a larger head, a slightly longer neck and rounded tail. Look for squared tail to help identify the Sharp-shinned Hawk.

Stan's Notes: A common hawk of backyards, parks and woodlands. Constructs its nest with sticks, usually high in a tree. Typically seen swooping in on birds visiting feeders and chasing them as they flee. Its short wingspan and long tail help it to maneuver through thick stands of trees in pursuit of prey. Calls a loud, high-pitched "kik-kik-kik-kik." Named "Sharp-shinned" for the sharp projection (keel) on the leading edge of its shin. A bird's shin is actually below the ankle (rather than above it, like ours) on the tarsus bone of its foot. In most birds, the tarsus bone is round, not sharp.

YEAR-ROUND

Eurasian Collared-Dove
Streptopelia decaocto

Size: 12½" (32 cm)

Male: Head, neck, breast and belly are gray-to-tan. Back, wings and tail are slightly darker. Thin black collar with a white border on the nape of neck. Tail is long and squared.

Female: same as male

Juvenile: similar to adult

Nest: platform; female and male build; 2–3 broods per year

Eggs: 3–5; cream-white without markings

Incubation: 12–14 days; female and male incubate

Fledging: 12–14 days; female and male feed the young

Migration: non-migrator

Food: seeds; will visit ground and seed feeders

Compare: Mourning Dove (pg. 151) is slightly smaller and darker. The Rock Pigeon (pg. 229) has colorful iridescent patches. Look for the black collar on the nape and the squared tail to help identify the Eurasian Collared-Dove.

Stan's Notes: A non-native bird. Moved into Florida in the 1980s after inadvertent introduction to the Bahamas. It reached Michigan and other northern states in the late 1990s. It has been expanding its range across North America and is predicted to spread just like it did through Europe from Asia. Unknown how this "new" bird will affect populations of the native Mourning Dove. Nearly identical to the Ringed Turtle-Dove, a common pet bird. The dark mark on the back of the neck gave rise to the common name. Look for flashes of white in the tail and dark wing tips when it lands or takes off.

YEAR-ROUND

Rock Pigeon
Columba livia

Size: 13" (33 cm)

Male: No set color pattern. Shades of gray-to-white with patches of gleaming, iridescent green-and-blue. Often has a light rump patch.

Female: same as male

Juvenile: same as adult

Nest: platform; female builds; 3–4 broods per year

Eggs: 1–2; white without markings

Incubation: 18–20 days; female and male incubate

Fledging: 25–26 days; female and male feed the young

Migration: non-migrator

Food: seeds, fruit; visits ground and seed feeders

Compare: Eurasian Collared-Dove (pg. 227) has a black collar on the nape. Mourning Dove (pg. 151) is smaller, light brown and lacks the variety of color combinations of the Rock Pigeon.

Stan's Notes: Also known as Domestic Pigeon. Formerly known as Rock Dove. Introduced to North America from Europe by the early settlers. Most common around cities and barnyards, where it scratches for seeds. One of the few birds with a wide variety of colors, produced by years of selective breeding while in captivity. Parents feed the young a regurgitated liquid known as crop-milk for the first few days of life. One of the few birds that can drink without tilting its head back. Nests under bridges or on buildings, balconies, barns and sheds. Was once thought to be a nuisance in cities and was poisoned. Now, many cities have Peregrine Falcons feeding on Rock Pigeons, which keeps their numbers in check.

soaring

juvenile

YEAR-ROUND
SUMMER

Cooper's Hawk
Accipiter cooperii

Size: 14–20" (36–51 cm); up to 3-ft. wingspan

Male: Medium-sized hawk with short wings and a long, rounded tail with several black bands. Slate-gray back, rusty breast, dark wing tips. Gray bill with a bright yellow spot at the base. Dark red eyes.

Female: similar to male, only larger

Juvenile: brown back, brown streaking on the breast, bright yellow eyes

Nest: platform; male and female build; 1 brood per year

Eggs: 2–4; greenish with brown markings

Incubation: 32–36 days; female and male incubate

Fledging: 28–32 days; male and female feed the young

Migration: non-migrator to partial, to the southern half of the L.P., southern states and Mexico

Food: small birds, mammals

Compare: The Sharp-shinned Hawk (pg. 225) is much smaller, lighter gray and has a squared tail. Look for the banded, rounded tail to help identify the Cooper's Hawk.

Stan's Notes: Found in many habitats, from woodlands to parks and backyards. Stubby wings help it to navigate around trees while it chases small birds. Will ambush prey, flying into heavy brush or even running on the ground in pursuit. Comes to feeders, hunting for birds. Flies with long glides followed by a few quick flaps. Calls a loud, clear "cack-cack-cack-cack." The young have gray eyes that turn bright yellow at 1 year and turn dark red later, after 3–5 years.

juvenile

in-flight
juvenile

in flight

Peregrine Falcon
Falco peregrinus

YEAR-ROUND
SUMMER

Size: 16–20" (41–51 cm); up to 3¾-ft. wingspan

Male: Dark gray back, dark "hood" head marking, wide black mustache and tan-to-white chest. Horizontal bars on belly, legs and undertail. Yellow base of bill, eye-ring and legs.

Female: similar to male, only noticeably larger

Juvenile: overall darker than adults, heavy streaking on the chest and belly

Nest: ground (scrape), on a cliff edge, tall building, bridge or smokestack; 1 brood per year

Eggs: 3–4; white, some with brown markings

Incubation: 29–32 days; female and male incubate

Fledging: 35–42 days; male and female feed the young

Migration: complete, to southern states, Mexico, Central and South America; some don't migrate

Food: birds (Rock Pigeons in cities, shorebirds and waterfowl in rural areas)

Compare: American Kestrel (pg. 141) is smaller and has two vertical black stripes on its face. Look for the dark "hood" head marking and mustache marks to help identify the Peregrine Falcon.

Stan's Notes: A wide-bodied raptor that hunts many bird species. The larger females hunt larger prey. Lives in many cities, diving (stooping) on pigeons at speeds up to 200 mph (322 kph), which knocks them to the ground. Soars with its wings flat, often riding thermals. During courtship, the male brings food to the female and performs aerial displays. Likes to nest on a high ledge or platform for a good view of its territory. A solitary nester and monogamous.

female
pg. 179

male

soaring

Northern Harrier
Circus cyaneus

Size: 18–22" (45–56 cm); up to 4-ft. wingspan

YEAR-ROUND
SUMMER

Male: A slender, low-flying hawk. Silver-gray with a large white rump patch and white belly. Long tail with faint narrow bands. Black wing tips. Yellow eyes.

Female: dark brown back, brown streaking on breast and belly, large white rump patch, thin black tail bands, black wing tips, yellow eyes

Juvenile: similar to female, with an orange chest

Nest: ground; female and male construct; 1 brood per year

Eggs: 4–8; bluish-white without markings

Incubation: 31–32 days; female incubates

Fledging: 30–35 days; male and female feed the young

Migration: complete, to southern states, Mexico and Central America; some don't migrate

Food: mice, snakes, insects, small birds

Compare: Cooper's Hawk (pg. 231) has a rusty breast. Look for a low-gliding hawk with a large white rump patch to identify the male Harrier.

Stan's Notes: One of the easiest of hawks to identify. Glides just aboveground, following the contours of the land while searching for prey. Holds its wings just above the horizontal position, tilting back and forth in the wind, similar to Turkey Vultures. Formerly called Marsh Hawk due to its habit of hunting over marshes. Feeds and nests on the ground. Will also preen and rest on the ground. Unlike other hawks, mainly uses its hearing to find prey, followed by eyesight. At any age, it has a distinctive owl-like face disk.

in flight

Canada Goose
Branta canadensis

Size: 25–43" (64–109 cm); up to 5½-ft. wingspan

Male: Large gray goose with a black neck and head, and a white chin and cheek strap.

Female: same as male

Juvenile: same as adult

Nest: platform, on the ground; female constructs; 1 brood per year

Eggs: 5–10; white without markings

Incubation: 25–30 days; female incubates

Fledging: 42–55 days; male and female teach the young to feed

Migration: non-migrator to partial, to the L.P. and southern states; will move to places with open water

Food: aquatic plants, insects, seeds

Compare: Rarely confused with any other bird.

Stan's Notes: Eliminated from Michigan in the 1900s. Reintroduced to federal refuges in the 1930s and to local and state lands in the 1960–70s. Calls a classic "honk-honk-honk," especially during flight. Flocks fly in a large V when traveling long distances. Starts to breed in the third year. Adults mate for many years. If threatened, they will hiss as a warning. Males stand as sentinels at the edge of their group and will bob their heads and become aggressive if approached. Adults molt their primary flight feathers while raising their young, rendering family groups temporarily flightless. Several subspecies occur in the U.S. Generally eastern groups are paler than the western. Their size also varies, decreasing northward. The smallest subspecies is in the Arctic.

in flight

SUMMER

Great Blue Heron
Ardea herodias

Size: 42–48" (107–122 cm); up to 6-ft. wingspan

Male: Tall gray heron. Black eyebrows end in a few long plumes at the back of head. Long yellow bill. Long feathers at the base of neck drop down in a kind of necklace. Long legs.

Female: same as male

Juvenile: same as adult, but more brown than gray, a black crown and lacks plumes

Nest: platform, in a colony; male and female build; 1 brood per year

Eggs: 3–5; blue-green without markings

Incubation: 27–28 days; female and male incubate

Fledging: 56–60 days; male and female feed the young

Migration: complete, to southern states, Mexico, Central and South America

Food: small fish, frogs, insects, snakes, baby birds

Compare: Green Heron (pg. 247) is much smaller and has a short neck. Sandhill Crane (pg. 241) has a red cap. Look for the long yellow bill to help identify the Great Blue Heron.

Stan's Notes: The tallest and most common heron in Michigan. It is found in open water, from small ponds to large lakes. Stalks small fish in shallow water. Strikes at mice, squirrels and nearly anything it comes across. Red-winged Blackbirds will attack it to prevent or stop it from taking their babies out of their nests. In flight, holds its neck in an S shape and slightly cups its wings, while the legs trail straight out behind. Nests in a colony of up to 100 birds. Nests in trees near or hanging over water. Barks like a dog when startled.

in flight

in-flight
rusty stain

rusty
stain

Sandhill Crane

Antigone canadensis

SUMMER

Size: 42–48" (107–122 cm); up to 7-ft. wingspan

Male: Elegant gray crane with long legs and neck. Wings and body often rust-brown from mud staining. Scarlet-red cap. Yellow-to-red eyes.

Female: same as male

Juvenile: dull brown with yellow eyes; lacks a red cap

Nest: ground; female and male construct; 1 brood per year

Eggs: 2; olive with brown markings

Incubation: 28–32 days; female and male incubate

Fledging: 65 days; female and male feed the young

Migration: complete, to southern states and Mexico

Food: insects, fruit, worms, plants, amphibians

Compare: Great Blue Heron (pg. 239) has a longer bill and holds its neck in an S shape during flight. Look for the scarlet-red cap to help identify the Sandhill Crane.

Stan's Notes: One of the tallest birds in Michigan. Preens mud into its feathers, staining its plumage rust-brown (see insets). Gives a very loud and distinctive rattling call, often heard before the bird is seen. Flight is characteristic, with a faster upstroke, making the wings look like they're flicking in flight. Can fly at great heights of over 10,000 feet (3,050 m). Found in wetlands and often seen in large undisturbed fields close to water. Nests on the ground in a large mound of aquatic vegetation. Performs a spectacular mating dance. The birds will face each other, then bow and jump into the air while making loud cackling sounds and flapping their wings. They will also flip sticks and grass into the air during their dance.

male

female

SUMMER

Ruby-throated Hummingbird
Archilochus colubris

Size: 3–3½" (7.5–9 cm)

Male: Tiny iridescent green bird. Black throat patch reflects bright ruby-red in direct sunlight.

Female: same as male, but lacks a throat patch

Juvenile: same as female

Nest: cup; female builds; 1–2 broods per year

Eggs: 2; white without markings

Incubation: 12–14 days; female incubates

Fledging: 14–18 days; female feeds the young

Migration: complete, to southern states, Mexico and Central America

Food: nectar, insects; will come to nectar feeders

Compare: No other bird is as tiny. The Sphinx Moth also hovers at flowers, but it has clear wings, doesn't hum in flight, moves much slower than the Ruby-throat and can be approached.

Stan's Notes: This is the smallest bird in the state. Can fly straight up, straight down, backward, or hover in midair. Does not sing but will chatter or buzz to communicate. Weighing about the same as a U.S. penny, it takes about five average-sized hummingbirds to equal the weight of one chickadee. The wings create the humming sound. Flaps 50–60 times or more per second when flying at top speed. Breathes 250 times per minute. Heart beats up to 1,260 times per minute. Builds a stretchy nest with plant material and spiderwebs, gluing pieces of lichen to the exterior for camouflage. Attracted to colorful tubular flowers. Will extract and eat insects trapped in spiderwebs. A long-distance migrator, wintering in the tropics of Central America.

female
pg. 171

male

Wood Duck
Aix sponsa

SUMMER

Size: 17–20" (43–51 cm)

Male: A small, highly ornamented dabbling duck with a mostly green head and crest patterned with black-and-white, a rusty chest, white belly and red eyes.

Female: brown duck with a bright white eye-ring, a not-so-obvious crest and blue patch on wings (speculum), often hidden

Juvenile: similar to female

Nest: cavity; female lines an old woodpecker cavity or a nest box in a tree; 1 brood per year

Eggs: 10–15; cream-white without markings

Incubation: 28–36 days; female incubates

Fledging: 56–68 days; female teaches the young to feed

Migration: complete, to southern states

Food: aquatic insects, plants, seeds

Compare: More colorful than the male Green-winged Teal (pg. 159). Lacks the large wide bill of the male Northern Shoveler (pg. 251).

Stan's Notes: A common duck of quiet, shallow backwater ponds. Nearly went extinct around 1900 due to overhunting, but it's doing well now. Nests in a tree cavity or a nest box in a tree. Seen flying in forests or perching on high branches. Female takes off with a loud squealing call and enters the nest cavity from full flight. Lays some eggs in a neighboring nest (egg dumping), resulting in excess of 20 eggs in some clutches. Hatchlings stay in the nest for 24 hours, then jump from as high up as 60 feet (18 m) to the ground or water to follow their mother. They never return to the nest.

Green Heron
Butorides virescens

Size: 16–22" (41–56 cm)

Male: Short and stocky heron. Blue-green back and rust-red neck and breast. Dark green crest. Short legs are normally yellow but turn bright orange during the breeding season.

Female: same as male

Juvenile: similar to adult, with a bluish-gray back and white-streaked breast and neck

Nest: platform; female and male build; 2 broods per year

Eggs: 2–4; light green without markings

Incubation: 21–25 days; female and male incubate

Fledging: 35–36 days; female and male feed the young

Migration: complete, to southern states, Mexico, Central and South America

Food: small fish, aquatic insects, small amphibians

Compare: Great Blue Heron (pg. 239) is larger and has long legs. Look for a small heron with a green back and crest to identify the Green Heron.

Stan's Notes: Often gives an explosive, rasping "skyew" call when startled. Holds its head close to its body, which sometimes makes it look like it doesn't have a neck. Makes short, quick flights across the water. Waits on the shore or wades stealthily, hunting for small fish, aquatic insects and small amphibians. Places an object, such as an insect, on the water's surface to attract fish to catch. Raises its crest when excited. Nests in a tall tree, often a short distance from the water. The nest can be very high up in the tree. Babies give a loud ticking sound, like the ticktock of a clock.

female
pg. 175

male

Mallard
Anas platyrhynchos

SUMMER

Size: 19–21" (48–53 cm)

Male: A large, bulbous green head, white necklace and rust-brown or chestnut chest. Gray-and-white sides. Yellow bill. Orange legs and feet.

Female: brown duck with an orange-and-black bill and blue-and-white wing mark (speculum)

Juvenile: same as female, but with a yellow bill

Nest: ground; female builds; 1 brood per year

Eggs: 7–10; greenish-to-whitish, unmarked

Incubation: 26–30 days; female incubates

Fledging: 42–52 days; female leads the young to food

Migration: complete, to southern states; some stay in Michigan and do not migrate

Food: seeds, plants, aquatic insects; will come to ground feeders offering corn

Compare: Most people recognize this common duck. Male Northern Shoveler (pg. 251) has a white chest with rusty sides and a very large, spoon-shaped bill. Look for the green head and yellow bill to identify the male Mallard.

Stan's Notes: A familiar dabbling duck of lakes and ponds. Also found in rivers, streams and some backyards. Tips forward to feed on vegetation on the bottom of shallow water. The name "Mallard" comes from the Latin word *masculus,* meaning "male," referring to the male's habit of taking no part in raising the young. Male and female have white underwings and white tails, but only the male has black central tail feathers that curl upward. Unlike the female, the male doesn't quack. Returns to its birthplace each year.

female
pg. 177

male

MIGRATION

Northern Shoveler
Spatula clypeata

Size: 19–21" (48–53 cm)

Male: Medium-sized duck with an iridescent green head, rust sides, white chest. Extraordinarily large, spoon-shaped bill, almost always held pointed toward the water.

Female: brown and black all over, green wing patch (speculum) and a large spoon-shaped bill

Juvenile: same as female

Nest: ground; female builds; 1 brood per year

Eggs: 9–12; olive without markings

Incubation: 22–25 days; female incubates

Fledging: 30–60 days; female leads the young to food

Migration: complete, to southern states, Mexico and Central America

Food: aquatic insects, plants

Compare: Male Mallard (pg. 249) is similar, but it lacks the large spoon-shaped bill. The male Wood Duck (pg. 245) is smaller and has a crest.

Stan's Notes: One of several species of shovelers. Called "Shoveler" due to the peculiar, shovel-like shape of its bill. Given the common name "Northern" because it is the only species of these ducks in North America. Seen in shallow wetlands, ponds and small lakes in flocks of 5–10 birds. Flocks fly in tight formation. Swims low in water, pointing its large bill toward the water as if it's too heavy to lift. Usually swims in tight circles while feeding. Feeds mainly by filtering tiny aquatic insects and plants from the surface of the water with its bill. Female gathers plant material and forms it into a nest a short distance from the water.

in flight

female
pg. 271

male

Common Merganser
Mergus merganser

SUMMER
MIGRATION
WINTER

Size: 26–28" (66–71 cm)

Male: Long, thin, duck-like bird with a green head and black back. White sides, chest and neck. Long, pointed orange bill. Often looks black-and-white in poor light.

Female: same size and shape as the male, with a rust-red head and ragged "hair," gray body with a white chest and chin

Juvenile: same as female

Nest: cavity; female lines an old woodpecker hole or a natural cavity; 1 brood per year

Eggs: 9–11; ivory without markings

Incubation: 28–33 days; female incubates

Fledging: 70–80 days; female feeds the young

Migration: complete, to southern states, Mexico and Central America

Food: small fish, aquatic insects, amphibians

Compare: Male Mallard (pg. 249) is smaller and lacks the black back and long, pointed orange bill.

Stan's Notes: Seen on any open water during the winter but more common along large rivers than lakes. A large, shallow water diver that feeds on fish in 10–15 feet (3–4.5 m) of water. Bill has a fine, serrated-like edge that helps catch slippery fish. Female often lays some eggs in other merganser nests (egg dumping), resulting in up to 15 young in some broods. Male leaves the female once she starts incubating. Orphans are accepted by other merganser mothers with young. Fast flight, often low and close to the water, in groups but not in formation. Usually not vocal except for an alarm call.

female
pg. 291

male

SUMMER

American Redstart
Setophaga ruticilla

Size: 5" (13 cm)

Male: A striking black warbler with orange patches on the sides, wings and tail. White belly.

Female: olive-brown with yellow patches on the sides, wings and tail, white belly

Juvenile: same as female; male attains orange tinges in the second year

Nest: cup; female builds; 1 brood per year

Eggs: 3–5; off-white with brown markings

Incubation: 12 days; female incubates

Fledging: 9 days; female and male feed the young

Migration: complete, to Mexico, Central America and South America

Food: insects, seeds, occasionally berries

Compare: The male Baltimore Oriole (pg. 257) and male Red-winged Blackbird (pg. 29) are much larger. The male American Redstart is the only small black-and-orange bird flitting around the top of trees.

Stan's Notes: This warbler is common and widespread in Michigan. Found in woodlands, forest edges, parks and yards. Prefers large, unbroken tracts of forest. Appears to be hyperactive when it feeds, hovering and darting back and forth to glean insects from leaves. Often droops wings and fans tail before launching out to catch an insect. Look for the flashing black-and-orange colors of the male high up in trees. First-year males have yellow markings and look like the females. Sings a high-pitched song that builds in intensity, and then suddenly ends.

female
pg. 297

male

SUMMER

Baltimore Oriole
Icterus galbula

Size: 7–8" (18–20 cm)

Male: Flaming orange oriole with a black head and back. White-and-orange wing bars. Orange-and-black tail. Gray bill and dark eyes.

Female: pale yellow with orange tones, gray-brown wings, white wing bars, gray bill, dark eyes

Juvenile: same as female

Nest: pendulous; female builds; 1 brood per year

Eggs: 4–5; bluish with brown markings

Incubation: 12–14 days; female incubates

Fledging: 12–14 days; female and male feed the young

Migration: complete, to Mexico, Central America and South America

Food: insects, fruit, nectar; comes to nectar, orange half and grape jelly feeders

Compare: Male American Redstart (pg. 255) has much less orange. Male Orchard Oriole (pg. 259) is much darker orange. Look for the flaming orange to identify the male Baltimore Oriole.

Stan's Notes: A fantastic songster, often heard before seen. Easily attracted to a bird feeder that offers sugar water (nectar), orange halves or grape jelly. Parents bring their young to feeders. Sits at the top of trees, feeding on caterpillars. Female builds a sock-like nest at the outermost branches of tall trees. Prefers parks, yards and forests and often returns to the same area year after year. Seen during migration and summer. Some of the last birds to arrive in spring (May) and first to leave in the fall (September). Young males turn orange-and-black at 1½ years of age.

female
pg. 299

male

first-year
male

SUMMER

Orchard Oriole
Icterus spurius

Size: 7–8" (18–20 cm)

Male: Dark orange oriole with a black head, throat, upper back, wings and tail. White wing bar. Bill is long and thin. Gray mark on lower bill.

Female: olive-green back, dull yellow belly and gray wings with two indistinct white wing bars

Juvenile: same as female; first-year male looks like the female with a black bib

Nest: pendulous; female builds; 1 brood per year

Eggs: 3–5; pale blue-to-white, brown markings

Incubation: 11–12 days; female and male incubate

Fledging: 11–14 days; female and male feed the young

Migration: complete, to Mexico, Central America and northern South America

Food: insects, fruit, nectar; comes to nectar, orange half and grape jelly feeders

Compare: The male Baltimore Oriole (pg. 257) is brighter orange. The male American Redstart (pg. 255) has a white belly. Look for the dark orange plumage to identify the male Orchard Oriole.

Stan's Notes: Named "Orchard" for its preference for orchards. Also likes open woods. Eats insects until wild fruit starts to ripen. Often nests alone; sometimes nests in small colonies. Parents bring their young to bird feeding stations after they fledge. Many people don't see these birds at their feeders very much during the summer and think they have left, but the birds are still there, hunting for insects to feed to their young. Some of the first birds to migrate at the end of summer. Often migrates in flocks with Baltimore Orioles.

male

female
pg. 99

yellow
male

House Finch
Haemorhous mexicanus

YEAR-ROUND

Size: 5" (13 cm)

Male: Small finch with a red-to-orange face, throat, chest and rump. Brown cap. Brown marking behind eyes. White belly with brown streaks. Brown wings with white streaks.

Female: brown with a heavily streaked white chest

Juvenile: similar to female

Nest: cup, occasionally in a cavity, female builds; 2 broods per year

Eggs: 4–5; pale blue, lightly marked

Incubation: 12–14 days; female incubates

Fledging: 15–19 days; female and male feed the young

Migration: non-migrator to partial; will move around to find food

Food: seeds, fruit, leaf buds; visits seed feeders and feeders that offer grape jelly

Compare: The male Purple Finch (pg. 263) has a red cap. The male Pine Grosbeak (pg. 269) has dark wings with a smattering of gray. Look for the brown cap and streaked belly to help identify the male House Finch.

Stan's Notes: Can be a common bird at your feeders. A very social bird, visiting feeders in small flocks. Likes to nest in hanging flower baskets. Male sings a loud, cheerful warbling song. It was originally introduced to Long Island, New York, from the western U.S. in the 1940s. Now found throughout the country. Suffers from a disease that causes the eyes to crust, resulting in blindness and death. Rarely, some males are yellow (see inset), perhaps due to poor diet.

female
pg. 115

male

YEAR-ROUND
WINTER

Purple Finch
Haemorhous purpureus

Size: 6" (15 cm)

Male: Raspberry-red head, cap, chest, back and rump. Brownish wings and tail. Large bill.

Female: heavily streaked brown-and-white bird with bold white eyebrows

Juvenile: same as female

Nest: cup; female and male build; 1 brood per year

Eggs: 4–5; greenish-blue with brown markings

Incubation: 12–13 days; female incubates

Fledging: 13–14 days; female and male feed the young

Migration: irruptive; moves around in winter to find food

Food: seeds, insects, fruit; comes to seed feeders

Compare: The male House Finch (pg. 261) has a brown cap and a streaked belly. Male Pine Grosbeak (pg. 269) is much larger and has gray on its wings. Look for the raspberry-red cap to help identify the male Purple Finch.

Stan's Notes: Found year-round in the northern half of Michigan and during winter in the southern half of the L.P. An irruptive migrator, more common in some parts of the state, but not always seen every winter. Travels in flocks of up to 50 birds. Visits seed feeders along with House Finches, which makes it hard to tell them apart. Ash tree seeds are an important source of food; feeds mainly on seeds. Found in coniferous forests, mixed woods, woodland edges and suburban backyards. Flies in the typical undulating, up-and-down pattern of finches. Sings a rich, loud song. Gives a distinctive "tic" note only in flight. The male is not purple. The Latin species name *purpureus* means "purple" or other reddish colors.

female
pg. 295

male

SUMMER

Scarlet Tanager
Piranga olivacea

Size: 7" (18 cm)

Male: Bright scarlet-red bird with coal-black wings and tail. Ivory bill and dark eyes.

Female: drab greenish-yellow bird with olive wings and tail, whitish wing linings and dark eyes

Juvenile: same as female

Nest: cup; female builds; 1 brood per year

Eggs: 4–5; blue-green with brown markings

Incubation: 13–14 days; female incubates

Fledging: 9–11 days; female and male feed the young

Migration: complete, to Central and South America

Food: insects, fruit

Compare: Male Northern Cardinal (pg. 267) is larger, with a black mask and red bill. Look for the black wings and tail to help identify the male Scarlet Tanager.

Stan's Notes: A tropical-looking bird. Found in mature deciduous woodlands, where it hunts for insects high up in trees. Requires a territory covering at least 4 acres (1.5 ha) for nesting but prefers 8 acres (3 ha). Arrives late in spring and leaves early in fall. Both the male and female sing like American Robins, but the tanagers intersperse an unusual "chick-burr" call in their songs. The song of the female is like that of the male's, only softer. This bird is one of hundreds of tanager species in the world. Nearly all are brightly colored and live in the tropics. The name "Tanager" comes from a South American Tupi Indian word meaning "any small, brightly colored bird." The male sheds (molts) his bright scarlet plumage in the fall, appearing more like the female during winter.

female
pg. 135

male

juvenile

Northern Cardinal
Cardinalis cardinalis

YEAR-ROUND

Size: 8–9" (20–23 cm)

Male: Red bird with a black mask that extends from the face to the throat. Large crest and large red bill.

Female: buff-brown with a black mask, large reddish bill, and red tinges on the crest and wings

Juvenile: same as female, but with a blackish-gray bill

Nest: cup; female builds; 2–3 broods per year

Eggs: 3–4; bluish-white with brown markings

Incubation: 12–13 days; female and male incubate

Fledging: 9–10 days; female and male feed the young

Migration: non-migrator

Food: seeds, insects, fruit; comes to seed feeders

Compare: The male Scarlet Tanager (pg. 265) is smaller and has black wings. Look for the black mask, large crest and red bill to identify the male Northern Cardinal.

Stan's Notes: A familiar backyard bird. Seen in a variety of habitats, including parks. Usually likes thick vegetation. One of the few species in which both males and females sing. Can be heard all year. Listen for its "whata-cheer-cheer-cheer" territorial call in spring. Watch for a male feeding a female during courtship. The male also feeds the young of the first brood while the female builds a second nest. Territorial in spring, fighting its own reflection in a window or other reflective surface. Non-territorial in winter, gathering in small flocks of up to 20 birds. Makes short flights from cover to cover, often landing on the ground. *Cardinalis* denotes importance, as represented by the red priestly garments of Catholic cardinals.

female
pg. 215

male

Pine Grosbeak
Pinicola enucleator

WINTER

Size: 9" (23 cm)

Male: Plump rose-and-gray finch with a long dark tail. Dark wings smattered with gray. Two white wing bars. Short, pointed dark bill.

Female: mostly gray with dark wings and tail, head and rump have a dull yellow tinge

Juvenile: male has a touch of red on head and rump; female is similar to the adult female

Nest: cup; female builds; 1 brood per year

Eggs: 4–5; bluish-green without markings

Incubation: 13–15 days; female incubates

Fledging: 13–20 days; female and male feed the young

Migration: irruptive; moves around the U.P. and northern parts of the L.P. in winter to find food

Food: seeds, fruit, insects; will come to seed feeders

Compare: Male Purple Finch (pg. 263) and male House Finch (pg. 261) are much smaller. Look for the gray wings of the male Pine Grosbeak.

Stan's Notes: A very tame and approachable seed eater. Common in some winters and not so common in others. Often seen along roads or on the ground, eating tiny grains of sand and dirt, which help aid digestion. Favors coniferous woods, rarely moving out of coniferous regions during summer, but also likes mixed forests. Will bathe in fluffy snow. Flies in a typical finch-like undulating pattern while giving soft, whistle "cheer" calls. Male sings a rich, beautiful song all year long. Male and female develop a pouch in the bottom of their mouths (buccal pouch) during the breeding season for transporting seeds to their young.

in flight

male
pg. 253

female

Common Merganser

Mergus merganser

SUMMER
MIGRATION
WINTER

Size: 26–28" (66–71 cm)

Female: A long, thin, duck-like bird with a rust-red head and ragged "hair." Gray body and white chest and chin. Long, pointed orange bill.

Male: same size and shape as the female, but with a green head, black back and white sides

Juvenile: same as female

Nest: cavity; female lines an old woodpecker hole or a natural cavity; 1 brood per year

Eggs: 9–11; ivory without markings

Incubation: 28–33 days; female incubates

Fledging: 70–80 days; female feeds the young

Migration: complete, to southern states, Mexico and Central America

Food: small fish, aquatic insects

Compare: Hard to confuse with other birds. Look for a rust-red head with ragged "hair," a white chin and a long, pointed orange bill to identify.

Stan's Notes: Seen on any open water during the winter but more common along large rivers than lakes. A large, shallow water diver that feeds on fish in 10–15 feet (3–4.5 m) of water. Bill has a fine, serrated-like edge that helps catch slippery fish. Female often lays some eggs in other merganser nests (egg dumping), resulting in up to 15 young in some broods. Male leaves the female once she starts incubating. Orphans are accepted by other merganser mothers with young. Fast flight, often low and close to the water, in groups but not in formation. Usually not vocal except for an alarm call that sounds like a muffled quack.

in flight

SUMMER
MIGRATION

Common Tern
Sterna hirundo

Size: 13–16" (33–40 cm)

Male: White-and-gray tern with a jet-black crown. Red-orange bill with a black tip. Long, forked white "tern" tail. Red legs and feet. Tips of wings appear dark gray when seen in flight.

Female: same as male

Juvenile: similar to adult, with a blue-gray back and white-streaked chest and neck, incomplete brown-to-black crown

Nest: ground; female and male construct; 1 brood per year

Eggs: 1–3; olive-brown with brown markings

Incubation: 21–27 days; female and male incubate

Fledging: 26–27 days; female and male feed young

Migration: complete, to South America

Food: fish, aquatic insects

Compare: Smaller than Ring-billed Gull (pg. 275) and has a reddish-orange bill and a forked tail. Look for the jet-black crown and the black-tipped red-orange bill to help identify the Common Tern.

Stan's Notes: This tern was nearly eliminated from the state prior to 1900 due to plume hunting. Protected by 1910, it now has made a comeback. Catches small fish by diving into water headfirst. Will catch insects in flight. Arrives at nesting grounds during April. Nest is often in sand or pebbles and lined with grass, shells and aquatic plants. Nests in small colonies. Competition and predation from gulls and birds of prey keep the population from expanding.

in flight

breeding

juvenile

winter

Ring-billed Gull
Larus delawarensis

YEAR-ROUND
SUMMER
MIGRATION

Size: 18–20" (45–51 cm); up to 4-ft. wingspan

Male: A white bird with gray wings, black wing tips spotted with white, and a white tail, as seen in flight. Yellow bill with a black ring near the tip. Yellowish legs, feet. Winter plumage has a speckled brown back of head and nape of neck.

Female: same as male

Juvenile: brown speckles with a brown tip of tail and a mostly dark bill

Nest: ground; female and male construct; 1 brood per year

Eggs: 2–4; off-white with brown markings

Incubation: 20–21 days; female and male incubate

Fledging: 20–40 days; female and male feed the young

Migration: complete, to southern states and Mexico; non-migrator along the coasts in the L.P

Food: insects, fish; scavenges for food

Compare: The Herring Gull (pg. 277) has an orange-red mark on its lower bill and pinkish legs. Look for the black ring on the bill to help identify the Ring-billed Gull.

Stan's Notes: A common gull of garbage dumps and parking lots. This bird is expanding its range and remaining farther north longer in winter, where it is foraging for food in cities. A three-year gull with different plumages in each of its first three years. Attains the ring on its bill after the first winter and adult plumage in the third year. Defends a small area around the nest, usually only a few feet.

in flight

breeding

juvenile

winter

Herring Gull

Larus argentatus

YEAR-ROUND
SUMMER
MIGRATION

Size: 23–26" (58–66 cm); up to 5-ft. wingspan

Male: White bird with slate-gray wings. Black wing tips with tiny white spots. Yellow bill with an orange-red spot near the tip of the lower bill (mandible). Pinkish legs and feet. Winter plumage has gray speckles on head and neck.

Female: same as male

Juvenile: mottled brown-to-gray, with a black bill

Nest: ground; female and male construct; 1 brood per year

Eggs: 2–3; olive with brown markings

Incubation: 24–28 days; female and male incubate

Fledging: 35–36 days; female and male feed the young

Migration: complete, to southern states and Mexico; non-migrator along the coasts in the L.P.

Food: fish, insects, clams, eggs, baby birds

Compare: Ring-billed Gull (pg. 275) is smaller and has yellowish legs and feet, and a black ring on its bill. Look for the orange-red spot on the bill to help identify the Herring Gull.

Stan's Notes: A common gull of large lakes. An opportunistic bird, scavenging for human food in dumpsters, parking lots and other places with garbage. Takes eggs and young from other bird nests. Often drops clams and other shellfish from heights to break the shells and get to the soft interior. Nests in colonies, returning to the same site annually. Lines its nest with grass and seaweed. It takes about four years for the juveniles to obtain adult plumage. Adults have spotted heads during winter.

white
morph

blue morph

juvenile

in flight

MIGRATION

Snow Goose
Anser caerulescens

Size: 25–38" (64–97 cm); up to 4½-ft. wingspan

Male: White morph has black wing tips and varying patches of black-and-brown. Blue morph has a white head and a gray breast and back. Both morphs have a pink bill and legs.

Female: same as male

Juvenile: overall dull gray with a dark bill

Nest: ground; female builds; 1 brood per year

Eggs: 3–5; white without markings

Incubation: 23–25 days; female incubates

Fledging: 45–49 days; female and male teach the young to feed

Migration: complete, to southern states and Mexico

Food: aquatic insects and plants

Compare: The Tundra Swan (pg. 283) and Trumpeter Swan (pg. 285) lack black wing tips. The Canada Goose (pg. 237) has a black neck and white chin strap.

Stan's Notes: This bird occurs in light (white) and dark (blue) color morphs. The white morph is more common than the blue. A bird of wide-open fields, wetlands and lakes of any size. It has a thick, serrated bill, which helps it to grab and pull up plants. Breeds in large colonies on the northern tundra in Canada. Female starts to breed at 2–3 years. Older females produce more eggs and are more successful at reproduction than younger females. Migrates in huge flocks with thousands of birds. Has a classic goose-like call. When thousands of geese call, it sounds like one constant call.

in flight

Great Egret
Ardea alba

SUMMER
MIGRATION

Size: 36–40" (91–102 cm); up to 4½-ft. wingspan

Male: Tall, thin, elegant all-white bird with a long neck and a long, pointed yellow bill. Black stilt-like legs and black feet.

Female: same as male

Juvenile: same as adult

Nest: platform; male and female build; 1 brood per year

Eggs: 2–3; light blue without markings

Incubation: 23–26 days; female and male incubate

Fledging: 43–49 days; female and male feed the young

Migration: complete, to southern states, Mexico and Central America

Food: small fish, aquatic insects, frogs, crayfish

Compare: Smaller than the Great Blue Heron (pg. 239), but similar in shape. Look for the long, thin white neck and long, pointed yellow bill to help identify the Great Egret.

Stan's Notes: A graceful, stately bird. Slowly stalks shallow ponds, lakes and wetlands in search of small fish to spear with its long, sharp bill. Holds neck in an S shape during flight. Nests in colonies with as many as 100 birds. Gives a loud, dry croak if disturbed or when squabbling for a nest site at the colony. The name "Egret" comes from the French word *aigrette,* meaning "ornamental tufts of plumes." The plumes grow near the tail during the breeding season. Hunted to near extinction in the 1800s and early 1900s for its beautiful long plumes, which were used to decorate hats for women. Today, the egret is a protected species.

juvenile

in flight

MIGRATION

Tundra Swan
Cygnus columbianus

Size: 50–54" (127–137 cm); up to 5½-ft. wingspan

Male: All-white swan. Black bill, legs and feet. Small yellow mark in front of each eye (lore).

Female: same as male

Juvenile: same size as adult, with gray plumage and a pinkish-gray bill

Nest: ground; female and male construct; 1 brood per year

Eggs: 4–5; cream-white without markings

Incubation: 35–40 days; female and male incubate

Fledging: 60–70 days; female and male feed the young

Migration: complete, to the East Coast

Food: plants, aquatic insects

Compare: The Trumpeter Swan (pg. 285) is much larger and lacks yellow lores on its face. The Snow Goose (pg. 279) is much smaller and has black wing tips. Look for the black bill and legs to help identify the Tundra Swan.

Stan's Notes: Formerly called Whistling Swan. Named "Tundra" for its nesting habitat in Alaska. Migrates diagonally across North America to reach wintering grounds on the East Coast. Gathers in large numbers in some lakes and rivers to rest for a day or two, then continues to migrate. Usually seen only during fall migration; seen in some years during spring migration. Often in large family groups of 20 or more swans. Flies in large V formations. Gives a high-pitched, whistle-like call. Young are easily distinguished from the adults by their gray plumage and pinkish-gray bills. Hard to see the characteristic lores; often covered by mud or other debris.

in flight

juvenile

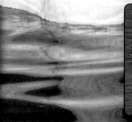

Mute Swan

SUMMER

Trumpeter Swan
Cygnus buccinator

Size: 58–62" (147–157 cm); up to 6½-ft. wingspan

Male: A large all-white swan with an all-black bill, legs and feet.

Female: same as male

Juvenile: same size as adult, with gray plumage and a pinkish-gray bill

Nest: ground; female and male construct; 1 brood per year

Eggs: 4–6; cream-white without markings

Incubation: 33–37 days; female incubates

Fledging: 100–120 days; female and male show the young what to eat

Migration: complete, to southern states

Food: aquatic plants, insects

Compare: The Tundra Swan (pg. 283) is very similar, but it has small yellow marks in front of its eyes (lores). Mute Swan (see inset) has an orange bill with a prominent black knob at the base. Snow Goose (pg. 279) is much smaller and has black wing tips.

Stan's Notes: Was once eliminated from the state due to market hunting, but it was reintroduced with great success. Reintroduced birds are identified by large colored tags on the neck or wings. Most breeding programs were started with eggs taken from Trumpeters in Alaska. Often on larger rivers. Also in wetlands, marshes, small lakes, ponds and farm fields. Mated pairs defend large territories and construct large mound nests at the edge of water. Named for its loud, trumpet-like call, typically given in flight.

winter male

male

female

American Goldfinch
Spinus tristis

YEAR-ROUND

Size: 5" (13 cm)

Male: Bright canary-yellow finch with a black fore-head and tail. Black wings with white wing bars. White rump. No markings on the chest. Winter male is similar to the female.

Female: dull olive-yellow plumage with brown wings; lacks a black forehead

Juvenile: same as female

Nest: cup; female builds; 1 brood per year

Eggs: 4–6; pale blue without markings

Incubation: 10–12 days; female incubates

Fledging: 11–17 days; female and male feed the young

Migration: partial to non-migrator; small flocks of up to 20 birds move around to find food

Food: seeds, insects; comes to seed feeders

Compare: The male Yellow Warbler (pg. 293) is yellow with orange streaks on its chest. Pine Siskin (pg. 97) has a streaked chest and belly and yellow wing bars. The female House Finch (pg. 99) and female Purple Finch (pg. 115) have heavily streaked chests.

Stan's Notes: A common backyard resident. Most often found in open fields, scrubby areas and woodlands. Enjoys Nyjer seed in feeders. Breeds in late summer. Lines its nest with the silky down from wild thistle. Almost always in small flocks. Twitters while it flies. Flight is roller coaster-like. Moves around to find adequate food during winter. Often called Wild Canary due to the male's canary-colored plumage. Male sings a pleasant, high-pitched song.

male

female

SUMMER

Common Yellowthroat
Geothlypis trichas

Size: 5" (13 cm)

Male: Olive-brown bird with a bright yellow throat and chest, white belly and distinctive black mask outlined in white. A long, thin, pointed black bill.

Female: similar to male, but lacks a black mask

Juvenile: same as female

Nest: cup; female builds; 2 broods per year

Eggs: 3–5; white with brown markings

Incubation: 11–12 days; female incubates

Fledging: 10–11 days; female and male feed the young

Migration: complete, to southern states, Mexico and Central America

Food: insects

Compare: Male Yellow Warbler (pg. 293) has orange streaking on its chest and lacks a mask. The male American Goldfinch (pg. 287) has a black forehead and wings. Yellow-rumped Warbler (pg. 201) only has patches of yellow and lacks the yellow chest of the Yellowthroat.

Stan's Notes: A common warbler of open fields and marshes, breeding throughout Michigan during summer. Sings a cheerful, well-known "witchity-witchity-witchity-witchity" song from deep within tall grasses. Male sings from prominent perches and while he hunts. He performs a curious courtship display, bouncing in and out of tall grass while singing a mating song. Female builds a nest low to the ground. Young remain dependent on their parents longer than most other warblers. A frequent cowbird host.

male
pg. 255

female

SUMMER

American Redstart
Setophaga ruticilla

Size: 5" (13 cm)

Female: Olive-brown warbler with yellow patches on the sides, wings and tail. White belly.

Male: black with orange patches on the sides, wings and tail, white belly

Juvenile: same as female; male attains orange tinges in the second year

Nest: cup; female builds; 1 brood per year

Eggs: 3–5; off-white with brown markings

Incubation: 12 days; female incubates

Fledging: 9 days; female and male feed the young

Migration: complete, to Mexico, Central America and South America

Food: insects, seeds, occasionally berries

Compare: Female Yellow-rumped Warbler (pg. 201) is similar, but it has a yellow patch on its rump. Look for yellow patches on the sides, wings and tail to help identify the female Redstart.

Stan's Notes: This warbler is common and widespread in Michigan. Found in woodlands, forest edges, parks and yards. Prefers large, unbroken tracts of forest. Appears to be hyperactive when it feeds, hovering and darting back and forth to glean insects from leaves. Often droops wings and fans tail before launching out to catch an insect. Look for the flashing black-and-orange colors of the male high up in trees. First-year males have yellow markings and look like the females. Sings a high-pitched song that builds in intensity, and then suddenly ends.

male

female

Yellow Warbler
Setophaga petechia

SUMMER

Size: 5" (13 cm)

Male: A yellow warbler with thin orange streaks on the chest and belly. Long, pointed dark bill.

Female: same as male, but lacks orange streaks

Juvenile: similar to female, only much duller

Nest: cup; female builds; 1 brood per year

Eggs: 4–5; white with brown markings

Incubation: 11–12 days; female incubates

Fledging: 10–12 days; female and male feed young

Migration: complete, to southern states, Mexico, Central America and South America

Food: insects

Compare: Yellow-rumped Warbler (pg. 201) has just patches of yellow. Male American Goldfinch (pg. 287) has a black forehead and wings. Female American Goldfinch (pg. 287) has white wing bars. Look for the orange streaks on the chest to identify the Yellow Warbler.

Stan's Notes: Common and widespread. Seen in shrubby areas close to water, gardens and backyards. Zooms around shrubs and shorter trees. A prolific insect eater, gleaning small caterpillars and other insects from tree leaves. Male sings loudly, flies off to grab a bug, and then starts singing again. The male is easier to see higher up in trees than the duller, less conspicuous female. Male sings a string of notes that sound like "sweet, sweet, sweet, I'm-so-sweet!" Begins to migrate south in July and is gone by August. Males arrive in spring 1–2 weeks before females to claim territories. Migrates at night in mixed flocks of warblers. Rests and feeds during the day.

female

male
pg. 265

SUMMER

Scarlet Tanager
Piranga olivacea

Size: 7" (18 cm)

Female: Drab greenish-yellow bird with olive wings and tail. Whitish wing linings. Dark eyes.

Male: bright scarlet-red bird with coal-black wings and tail, an ivory bill and dark eyes

Juvenile: same as female

Nest: cup; female builds; 1 brood per year

Eggs: 4–5; blue-green with brown markings

Incubation: 13–14 days; female incubates

Fledging: 9–11 days; female and male feed the young

Migration: complete, to Central and South America

Food: insects, fruit

Compare: The female Baltimore Oriole (pg. 297) has gray-brown wings. Female American Goldfinch (pg. 287) has white wing bars. Look for the olive wings to identify the female Tanager.

Stan's Notes: A tropical-looking bird. Found in mature deciduous woodlands, where it hunts for insects high up in trees. Requires a territory covering at least 4 acres (1.5 ha) for nesting but prefers 8 acres (3 ha). Arrives late in spring and leaves early in fall. Both the female and male sing like American Robins, but the tanagers intersperse an unusual "chick-burr" call in their songs. The song of the female is like that of the male's, only softer. This bird is one of hundreds of tanager species in the world. Nearly all are brightly colored and live in the tropics. The name "Tanager" comes from a South American Tupi Indian word meaning "any small, brightly colored bird." The male sheds (molts) his bright scarlet plumage in the fall, appearing more like the female during winter.

male
pg. 257

female

Baltimore Oriole

Icterus galbula

SUMMER

Size: 7–8" (18–20 cm)

Female: A pale yellow oriole with orange tones, gray-brown wings and white wing bars. Gray bill. Dark eyes.

Male: flaming orange with a black head and back, white-and-orange wing bars, an orange-and-black tail, gray bill and dark eyes

Juvenile: same as female

Nest: pendulous; female builds; 1 brood per year

Eggs: 4–5; bluish with brown markings

Incubation: 12–14 days; female incubates

Fledging: 12–14 days; female and male feed the young

Migration: complete, to Mexico, Central America and South America

Food: insects, fruit, nectar; comes to nectar, orange half and grape jelly feeders

Compare: Female Orchard Oriole (pg. 299) has a dull yellow belly. Look for the gray-brown wings to help identify the female Baltimore Oriole.

Stan's Notes: A fantastic songster, often heard before seen. Easily attracted to a bird feeder that offers sugar water (nectar), orange halves or grape jelly. Parents bring their young to feeders. Sits at the top of trees, feeding on caterpillars. Female builds a sock-like nest at the outermost branches of tall trees. Prefers parks, yards and forests and often returns to the same area year after year. Seen during migration and summer. Some of the last birds to arrive in spring (May) and first to leave in the fall (September). Young males turn orange-and-black at 1½ years of age.

male
pg. 259

female

first-year
male

Orchard Oriole

Icterus spurius

SUMMER

Size: 7–8" (18–20 cm)

Female: An olive-green oriole with a dull yellow belly. Gray wings with two indistinct white wing bars. Bill is long and thin, with a gray mark on the lower bill (mandible).

Male: dark orange with a black head, throat, upper back, wings and tail, one white wing bar

Juvenile: same as female; first-year male looks like the female with a black bib

Nest: pendulous; female builds; 1 brood per year

Eggs: 3–5; pale blue-to-white, brown markings

Incubation: 11–12 days; female and male incubate

Fledging: 11–14 days; female and male feed the young

Migration: complete, to Mexico, Central America and northern South America

Food: insects, fruit, nectar; comes to nectar, orange half and grape jelly feeders

Compare: Female Baltimore Oriole (pg. 297) has orange tones and more distinct wing bars. Female Scarlet Tanager (pg. 295) has a larger bill.

Stan's Notes: Named "Orchard" for its preference for orchards. Also likes open woods. Eats insects until wild fruit starts to ripen. Often nests alone; sometimes nests in small colonies. Parents bring their young to bird feeding stations after they fledge. Many people don't see these birds at their feeders very much during the summer and think they have left, but the birds are still there, hunting for insects to feed to their young. Some of the first birds to migrate at the end of summer. Often migrates in flocks with Baltimore Orioles.

male

female

juvenile

Evening Grosbeak
Coccothraustes vespertinus

Size: 8" (20 cm)

Male: A striking bird with bright yellow eyebrows, rump and belly. Black-and-white wings and tail. Dark, dirty yellow head and large, thick ivory-to-greenish bill.

Female: similar to male, with softer colors and a gray head and throat

Juvenile: similar to female, with a brown bill

Nest: cup; female builds; 1 brood per year

Eggs: 3–4; blue with brown markings

Incubation: 12–14 days; female incubates

Fledging: 13–14 days; female and male feed the young

Migration: irruptive; moves around in winter to find food

Food: seeds, insects, fruit; comes to seed feeders

Compare: The American Goldfinch (pg. 287) is closely related, but it is much smaller. Female Pine Grosbeak (pg. 215) has a dull yellow tinge on its head. Look for the yellow eyebrows and thick bill to identify the Evening Grosbeak.

Stan's Notes: One of the largest finches. Characteristic finch-like undulating flight. Uses its unusually large bill to crack seeds, its main food source. Often seen on gravel roads eating gravel, which provides minerals, salt and grit to grind the seeds it eats. Sheds the outer layer of its bill during spring, exposing a blue-green bill. Moves in flocks in winter, searching for food, often visiting feeders. More numerous in some years than others. Sometimes it is totally absent. Was once a common feeder bird. Population is estimated to have declined more than 80 percent over the past 50 years.

Western
Meadowlark

Eastern Meadowlark
Sturnella magna

SUMMER MIGRATION

Size: 9" (23 cm)

Male: A robin-shaped bird with a short tail, yellow chest and belly, brown back and a V-shaped black necklace. White outer tail feathers, best seen when flying away.

Female: same as male

Juvenile: same as adult

Nest: cup, on the ground in dense cover; female builds; 2 broods per year

Eggs: 3–5; white with brown markings

Incubation: 13–15 days; female incubates

Fledging: 11–12 days; female and male feed the young

Migration: complete, to southern states, Mexico and Central America

Food: insects, seeds

Compare: The Horned Lark (pg. 123) is smaller and lacks the yellow chest and belly. Look for a V-shaped black marking on the chest to help identify the Eastern Meadowlark.

Stan's Notes: A songbird of open grassy country, singing when perched and in flight. Given the name "Meadowlark" because it's a bird of meadows and sings like the larks of Europe. Best known for its wonderful flute-like, clear whistling song. Often seen perching on fence posts but will quickly dive into tall grass when approached. Sometimes domes its nest with dried grass. Not in the lark family. A member of the blackbird family, related to grackles and orioles. Western Meadowlark (see inset) is very similar but sings a different song. The map reflects the combined range of both species.

BIRDING ON THE INTERNET

Birding online is a great way to discover additional information and learn more about birds. These websites will assist you in your pursuit of birds. Web addresses sometimes change a bit, so if one no longer works, just enter the name of the group into a search engine to track down the new address.

Site	Address
eBird	https://ebird.org/home
American Birding Association	www.aba.org
Cornell Lab of Ornithology	www.birds.cornell.edu
Author Stan Tekiela's home page	www.naturesmart.com

CHECKLIST/INDEX BY SPECIES

Use the boxes to check the birds you've seen.

OBSERVATION NOTES

OBSERVATION NOTES

MORE FOR THE MIDWEST BY STAN TEKIELA

Identification Guides

Birds of Prey of the Midwest
Field Guide

Mammals of Michigan
Field Guide

Reptiles & Amphibians of
Minnesota, Wisconsin and
Michigan Field Guide

Trees of Michigan Field Guide

Wildflowers of Michigan
Field Guide

Children's Books

C is for Cardinal

Can You Count the Critters?

Critter Litter

The Kids' Guide to Birds
of Michigan

Children's Books:
Adventure Board Book Series

Floppers & Loppers

Paws & Claws

Peepers & Peekers

Snouts & Sniffers

Children's Books:
Wildlife Picture Books

Baby Bear Discovers the World

The Cutest Critter

Do Beavers Need Blankets?

Hidden Critters

Jump, Little Wood Ducks

Some Babies Are Wild

Super Animal Powers

What Eats That?

Whose Baby Butt?

Whose Butt?

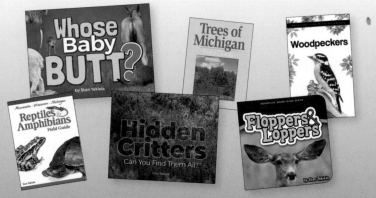

MORE FOR THE MIDWEST BY STAN TEKIELA

Audio CDs
Bird Songs of the Northwoods

Fascinating Loons: Alluring
Sounds of the Common Loon

Nature Books
Bird Trivia

Nature Smart

Start Mushrooming

A Year in Nature with Stan Tekiela

Notecards
Birds of the Heartland Notecards

Birds of the Northwoods
Notecards

Nature's Wild Cards
Birds of the Midwest
Playing Cards

Mammals of the Midwest
Playing Cards

Trees of the Midwest
Playing Cards

Wildflowers of the Midwest
Playing Cards

Hummingbirds Playing Cards

Loons Playing Cards

Raptors Playing Cards

ABOUT THE AUTHOR

Naturalist, wildlife photographer and writer Stan Tekiela is the originator of the popular state-specific field guide series that includes *Mammals of Michigan Field Guide*. Stan has authored more than 190 educational books, including field guides, quick guides, nature books, children's books, playing cards and more, presenting many species of animals and plants.

With a Bachelor of Science degree in Natural History from the University of Minnesota and as an active professional naturalist for more than 30 years, Stan studies and photographs wildlife throughout the United States and Canada. He has received various national and regional awards for his books and photographs. Also a well-known columnist and radio personality, his syndicated column appears in more than 25 newspapers, and his wildlife programs are broadcast on a number of Midwest radio stations. Stan can be followed on Facebook and Twitter. He can be contacted via www.naturesmart.com.

BIRD IDENTIFICATION FOR A NEW GENERATION

Stan Tekiela's famous *Birds of Michigan Field Guide* has delighted bird watchers for decades. Now, the award-winning author has written the perfect bird identification guide for children!

Book Features
- 86 common and important Michigan birds
- Species organized by color
- **BONUS:** Fun activities for the whole family to enjoy

This must-have beginner's guide is a perfect introduction to birding!